Bridget A. Burandt, LPC

JUNGIAN SPIRITUALITY

W9-BIS-057

THORSONS

PRINCIPLES

OF

JUNGIAN SPIRITUALITY

VIVIANNE CROWLEY

Thorsons

An Imprint of HarperCollinsPublishers

IN FOND MEMORY OF IAN AND SAM,
TO CHRIS AS ALWAYS,
AND TO BARBARA, ANITA, JOAN AND REYN,
MANY THANKS.

Thorsons
An Imprint of HarperCollins*Publishers*
77–85 Fulham Palace Road,
Hammersmith, London W6 8JB

Published by Thorsons 1998
1 3 5 7 9 10 8 6 4 2

Vivianne Crowley asserts the moral right to
be identified as the author of this work

A catalogue record for this book
is available from the British Library

ISBN 0 7225 3578 3

Text illustrations by Helen Elwes

Printed and bound in Great Britain by
Caledonian International Book Manufacturing Ltd, Glasgow

CONTENTS

INTRODUCTION

Vocatus atque non vocatus, Deus adherit.

(Called or not called, the God is there.)

FROM THE ORACLE AT DELPHI. WRITTEN ABOVE THE FRONT
DOOR OF JUNG'S HOME IN KÜSNACHT.

If you were to name some famous psychologists, two people might spring to mind – Sigmund Freud and Carl Jung. This book is about the latter.

Carl Jung lived for 86 years, born on 26 July 1875 and dying in 1961. Many of the terms that he invented or developed have entered our everyday vocabulary – archetypes, the collective unconscious, Persona, Anima, Animus, Shadow, Introversion, Extraversion. His life spanned most of the inventions that we now take for granted. He was born in the last quarter of the nineteenth century, the era of horse and carriage. Some of his last writings before he died were about UFOs. He was born into the nineteenth century; but was in every sense a modern man.

The nineteenth century was an era of vast upheaval in society and thought, in which old certainties were swept away. This was the scientific era of Darwin and his famous book *On the Origin of Species*. The literal teachings of Christianity were overturned by science. Evolution theory showed that the world was not created in seven days. It was not four thousand years old (about the length of then known recorded history), but millions, billions of years old. The human race itself was but a blip in time. What then was the life of an individual? We humans were no longer sure of our place in the scheme of things. We were no longer the chosen of the Judaeo-Christian God; destined to have dominion over all. Perhaps we were nothing but evolved apes.

Other adjustments were also required. Industrialization meant huge migrations of people into cities. The old ties to place, kin, clan and religious faith were broken. The nuclear family became the norm – mother, father and children living separately from grandparents. Now, in the West, the single-parent family and single-person households make up much of our society. The units become smaller; the individual is more separate and alone. Social disorganization, alienation, *anomie* and increased suicide rates are the penalties for the increased opportunities and material comfort that civilization brings.

In culture, the outcome of social change was a turning inward. People could no longer rely on the old religious certainties. They could trust only one thing – their own experience. New themes developed in art. Great art was no longer about historical and religious events. It celebrated the realm of the personal and of personal experience. Painting invited us to share the emotions of the artist. The symbolist movement of the late-nineteenth century began the journey inward. The surrealists of the twentieth century continued it. Literature was also turning to explore inner consciousness and the stream-of-consciousness novel was born. This was not a story, a narrative, but the outpourings of the writer's inner world and mind.

As the arts turned to the inner realm, so too did religion. It might seem that religion has always been about the inner world, but religion serves many functions. It can be a system for imposing morality and social control. It can provide sets of ritual actions that bind societies together. Often it is much more about society than about the individual. This is why the Pagan Roman Empire was so intolerant of Christianity. Everyone in the Empire was free to worship and believe in whatever deities they chose – providing they also paid honour to the Emperor, the representation of the Roman state and the unifying force within the Empire. Those who did not were political subversives. Christianity was a political crime, not a spiritual one.

Science had disproved the literal truth of many of the teachings of religion, but this did not necessarily mean an abandonment of spirituality. Those who were more aware saw that, freed of the shackles of superstitious doctrine, a new spiritual awareness might evolve; one based on our own spiritual experience. As materialism advanced, so many sought greater spiritual contact. Mysticism revived and the works of the Anglican female mystic Evelyn Underhill became popular. People turned to monastic spirituality, while rejecting orthodox Christianity; just as people today listen to Gregorian chant. While religion might not be literally true, it might symbolize a deeper truth – and the way to this truth lay within. Spiritual exploration was also taking place outside mainstream religion. The late-nineteenth century was the era of spiritualism, of psychic research, and of the great occult orders such as the Golden Dawn who sought to revive the knowledge of the Western Magical Tradition in a form suitable for the modern world. Many of the great thinkers and artists of the period were part of this esoteric revival. Others sought their inspiration in the East. In the nineteenth and twentieth centuries, empires were made and lost and East met West. The West went eastward and invaded and colonized the great civilizations and cultures of the Orient. Some of the colonialists were transformed by those they had colonized. They returned with the spirituality of the East. Sacred texts, teachings and teachers of Buddhism, Hinduism and Taoism journeyed westward.

In one of his last works, *The Undiscovered Self*,[1] Jung argued that the unifying force of Western culture had been the symbols and myths of religion. From the eighteenth century Age of Enlightenment onwards, we lost touch with these myths and symbols. Science helped us embrace the intellect but at the expense of the realm of feeling and spirit. The ancient path of mysticism was one way of reuniting ourselves with our myths and symbols. Another way was offered by a science of the new era – psychology and psychotherapy. Psychotherapy in its various forms – the examination of our fantasies, dreams and visions – could show us new symbols and new sources of renewal that conventional religion could no longer provide. For Jung, psychotherapy offered not just a means of reconciling ourselves with past trauma but a new way of approaching the goal of all spiritual traditions – unity with the divine. This, then, was Carl Jung's mission.

Carl Jung worked as a psychotherapist for nearly sixty years. His writings fill eighteen volumes. The books about him and his work fill whole bookcases in bookstores and libraries. All over the world, therapists train as Jungian analysts, and non-analysts meet to discuss his work. The wealth of literature about Jung and his thought is vast: Jung and the East, Jung and Christianity, Jung and Astrology, and Alchemy, and Gnosticism, and UFOs – the list is endless.

From UFOs – a scientific method of travelling to the stars – to the ancient art and science of astrology may seem a strange transition, but for Jung it was not. Above all, he was interested in the unknown – whether the depths of the unconscious mind, the mysterious and sometimes frightening world of mental illness, or the Gnostic sciences and the hidden mysteries of West and East. Some say he was a prophet, others a great psychologist, others a visionary, a guru, a charlatan, a dreamer. People loved him and worshipped him, or hated him and despised him. They were rarely neutral; which is why biographies are still being written today.

Jung's theories were grounded in great scholarship, but his psychology was essentially experiential. It drew on his own experiences, his career as a hospital psychiatrist working with the severely mentally ill, and case studies of hundreds of private patients, many of whom came to him for personal development and growth rather than because they were sick. It is a psychology that has inspired others and above all it is a psychology of the spirit. For the spiritual quest, the search for the divine, was something that absorbed Jung from his earliest years.

My own encounter with the work of Carl Jung began in late 1974. As a young student, I saw a book prominently displayed in Foyle's book store in London's book Mecca – Charing Cross Road. It had been reprinted the year before, forty years after its first publication. It was Jung's *Modern Man in Search of a Soul*. I read the book from cover to cover, understanding about a tenth of it. Much was beyond my life experience and understanding. What I did grasp though was that I was reading the work of a great mind.

In spring of that year, I had been in the Louvre in Paris standing in front of a painting by Kandinsky. Although I did not know it at the time, he was an artist whose paintings were designed to produce sudden realizations. I had such a 'bolt from the blue'. I knew suddenly that I did not want to study English at university as I had planned. I would study psychology, a subject I knew little about. In London, my interest was stimulated further by meeting someone who embodied Jung's archetype of the Wise Old Man. He was Sam Smith, a psychologist with the advertising agency Austin Knight and a member of the Board of Deputies, the organizing body for Judaism in Britain. Jung's book was a third encounter that confirmed my decision: I would become a psychologist.

I took a first degree at London University where I was disappointed to discover that Jung was mentioned hardly at all. After completing a doctorate, I decided to pursue a Jungian-oriented therapy training. I explored the option of full training as a Jungian analyst but was drawn to the more broadly-based and eclectic approach which I found through the Centre for Transpersonal Psychology; firstly through the work of Reyn and Joan Swallow, and then later through Barbara Somers and the late Ian Gordon-Brown. Here Jung's ideas were studied along with others. The work of Jung continues to inspire me and forms part of a series of workshops that my husband and I run on the *Psychology of the Sacred*. I also lecture on the psychology of religion at London University's King's College. This enables me to bring Jung into the undergraduate curriculum.

To approach Jung's work we must adopt the same open-minded approach as he did. The follower of Eastern mysticism will be frustrated by his focus on the West; the Christian will be alarmed at his excursion into the Western Magical Tradition; the Western esotericist will find his exploration of Christianity boring and distasteful; the rational psychologist will doubt the credibility of a man who could perform divination for patients beginning a course of therapy. Jung was wide-ranging and eclectic in his approach. This was deliberate. He was searching for universal truths and to find these he needed to explore all the spiritual traditions available to him. Reading Jung's work can be difficult. The ideas are complex and, since his writings span a period of around fifty years, they were continually evolving. This book is not exploration of the whole of Jung's psychology. The eighteen volumes of his *Collected Works* cannot be compressed into one slim paperback. It is Jung's work on spirituality that is the concern of this book: hence its title *Jungian Spirituality*. Inevitably, I have had to extract what I see as the vital essence of his thought. There is insufficient space for me to do justice to some of his writings. I have focused on his explorations of Buddhism, Hinduism, Taoism, Christianity and the Western Magical Tradition. I have not been able to cover his work on Islam, Judaism and the Classical Pagan mysteries, but I hope that what I have included here will be sufficient to be of value to those on a spiritual path who are seeking to fulfil the age-old maxim of the Mystery Traditions: To know thyself.

Vivianne Crowley
King's College, London
January 1998

NOTE

1 Carl G Jung (1957) *The Undiscovered Self (Present and Future)*, Princeton University Press, 1990 ed.

WHO WAS CARL JUNG?

Nobody could rid me of the conviction that it was enjoined upon me to do what God wanted, not what I wanted. That gave me strength to go my own way. Often I had the feeling that in all decisive matters I was no longer among men but was alone with God.

CARL JUNG AGED 15[1]

To understand Jung's approach to spirituality, we must first understand the man. Who was Carl Jung?

Carl Gustav Jung was born on 26 July 1875 in the German-speaking part of Switzerland. His family background spanned both medicine and the church. His paternal grandfather was a German doctor who moved to Switzerland in 1822 to become Professor of Surgery at the University of Basel. He became a well-known and respected citizen of Basel, eventually becoming Rector of the university. He also wrote plays. Family gossip had it that he was not really a 'Jung' at all; but the illegitimate son of the famous German literary genius Goethe, whom he resembled. Carl Jung's grandfather was born a Catholic, but in Basel, influenced by the famous theologian Friedrich Schleiermacher, he converted to Protestantism. He also became Grand Master of the Swiss Freemasons.

2

At that time most families were large. Carl Jung's father, Paul Achilles Jung (1842–1896), was his father's thirteenth child. Paul Jung did not follow his father into medicine but became a Protestant clergyman. It is not clear why he chose a career in the church, but it seems to have been a mistake and he never rose to high office. Carl Jung believed his father had never had a deep spiritual experience. For his father religion was a matter of doctrine and belief. One did not question, reason, or explore; one simply learned what the church taught and forced oneself to believe it. The denomination he belonged to was the Swiss Reformed Church. This taught that the basis for salvation was faith in the literal word of God as described in the Christian Bible – without faith one was damned.

The Reverend Paul Jung tried his best to live the life of a pious clergyman. He was greatly loved by the peasants and fishing families who were his parishioners, but his faith was precarious. He was wracked by continual doubts. These he tried to suppress, telling his son that, 'One must not think … one must believe.'[2] Paul Jung was trapped in a job that involved ministering to the spiritual needs of others when his own faith was in doubt. Given that to doubt was to be damned, this was frightening.

Paul Jung met his wife Emilie Preiswerk (1848–1923) at university when he was studying Hebrew with her father Samuel Preiswerk, a distinguished theologian who composed many hymns and religious poems. Although not himself Jewish, Samuel Preiswerk was a Zionist who strongly supported the idea of a Palestine homeland for the Jews. Emilie was the thirteenth child of Samuel Preiswerk's second wife.

Paul Jung and Emilie Preiswerk were both the products of respected bourgeois Basel families. On the surface it seemed they had much in common, but they were poles apart in personality. Emilie Jung was an earthy extravert who liked nothing better than to talk. Jung's father was an introverted intellectual. As a child Carl Jung's father taught him Latin and Christianity, but this was not the only religion he learned. In their Protestant parsonage beside the Rhine, his mother read him the myths of the Hindu deities.

In his early childhood, Carl Jung spent much time alone. His sister was not born until he was nine. In those pre-contraception days, this was an unusually small family and it was a reflection of the state of his parents' marriage: it was not good. Carl Jung's mother suffered from depression and from time to time she disappeared into hospital. From an early age, Carl Jung was aware of his mother's emotional problems and his father's spiritual problems. It is perhaps unsurprising that psychology and spirituality should become the two driving forces in his life.

Throughout his childhood and teens, Jung was preoccupied with trying to understand Christian religion. Teachings such as 'Original sin ' – the idea that humankind was estranged from God because first man, Adam, and first woman, Eve, had disobeyed him – were incomprehensible to Jung. If God was all-powerful, why did he arrange things so that Adam and Eve disobeyed? He could have prevented it; therefore he must have wanted them to sin. So serious were his musings that the boys at the Basel grammar school nick-named Jung 'Father Abraham' after the Biblical patriarch. This questioning led Jung to develop his own religious views, and they did not match those of his Church.

In the austere Swiss Reformed Church, the sermon was the centre of worship. Each Sunday Jung listened to his father's sermons with growing disillusionment. Despite his boredom, he prepared conscientiously for the ceremonies that marked his 'coming of age' in the Church – his confirmation and first communion. The communion experience was a sore disappointment.

Jung hoped for a religious revelation, a holy mystery. Instead, he found his neighbours dressed in frock coats and top hats. The communion service involved the mystical transformation of bread and wine into the body and blood of Jesus, the human incarnation of God. This was then eaten by the worshippers. For Jung, no magical transformation occurred. The bread stayed simply flat-tasting bread and the wine was thin and sour. It dawned on him that he had come to what was the pinnacle of religious initiation in the Church – and nothing had happened; nothing at all. The participants in the service had talked about God sure enough; but their words were empty. This did not damage Jung's belief in the divine. His own spiritual experiences convinced him that the divine was a reality, but he could find no trace of God in this ceremony. He knew that 'God could do stupendous things to me, things of fire and unearthly light; but this ceremony contained no trace of God – I had noticed nothing of the vast despair, overpowering elation and outpouring of grace which for me constituted the essence of God.'[3] He knew that he could never again participate in what seemed a hollow sham.

MEDICINE, PSYCHIATRY AND THE PARANORMAL

Jung was always interested in history. In his early youth, he thought of becoming an archaeologist. He also played with the idea of becoming a theologian; but was firmly discouraged by one of his clergyman uncles who recognized perhaps that young Carl was unlikely to cope with church orthodoxy. In the end, Jung followed in his paternal grandfather's footsteps and went to medical school.

Jung studied hard and managed to finish his medical training in five years. This was partly a matter of necessity. Jung's father died during his first year as a student and the family survived on Jung's part-time work, some commission he earned from selling antiques for an aunt, and handouts from relatives. Although he worked hard at his medical studies, on Sundays Jung found time to read philosophy – Kant, Goethe, Hartmann, Schopenhauer, Nietzsche. He also had more extravert fun-loving pursuits. In the evenings, he enjoyed himself. Sunday's philosophy sessions followed nights out at student clubs, where he drank so much beer he was known as 'The Barrel'. He seemed to be living out both his mother's earthy extravert enjoyment of life and his father's philosophical introversion.

Jung was keenly interested in what was the subject of considerable investigation at the end of the nineteenth century – psychical research. Jung first became interested in his teens when he found a book on the paranormal. The phenomena described sounded very like the ghost and spirit stories of the Swiss country folk that he had heard since childhood. He knew that there were similar tales from all over the world and became convinced that, whatever their origin, psychic phenomena were a regular occurrence in all societies. Those around him did not share his enthusiasm. They were disinterested or even fearful. He could not understand why people considered it preposterous that there might be events which broke the usual boundaries of time and space. He knew that animals could sense oncoming storms and earthquakes; that people had precognitive dreams that foretold death; that sometimes clocks stopped and glasses shattered when someone died. What had been commonplace in his country childhood was now ignored. He concluded that the urban world knew nothing of the real world, the rural world.

Although Jung may not have thought consciously about the paranormal until he read about it in a book, many of his mother's family were said to have 'the sight'. His grandfather Samuel

6   Preiswerk had visions and conversed with spirits. As a child, Jung's mother had to stand behind her father while he wrote his sermons to ensure that the spirits could not read over his shoulder. A chair was placed in his study for his dead first wife who was said to visit him regularly. Jung had paranormal experiences himself. In his teens, he saw an eighteenth-century carriage and began to have memories of a previous eighteenth-century life. He had some experiences of what is now called 'psychokinesis' – the ability to move material objects using the power of the mind. Today, this is being researched at Princeton University and evidence is emerging for its existence. Shortly after his father's death, when Jung was reading with his mother, there was a loud sound like a pistol crack in the room. The circular walnut table beside her split from the rim to beyond the centre. Two weeks later there was another phenomenon. Jung returned home to find his mother, fourteen-year-old sister and the maid agitated because another deafening crack had been heard coming from the direction of a nineteenth-century sideboard. Inside the sideboard Jung found that a bread knife blade had shattered into several pieces. He took the knife to a cutler who told them there were no faults in the steel. The cutler could offer no explanation of what had happened. A few weeks later Jung discovered that some of his mother's relatives were taking part in spiritualist seances. A fifteen-year-old cousin of his was acting as medium. Jung began attending and went to the sessions for two years. He stopped when his cousin's powers began to fade and she started to cheat. The experiences of the seances became the material for his doctoral dissertation.

When Jung came to revise for his final medical examinations, he left psychiatry until last. Jung's family had a long-standing interest in mental illness. His father was chaplain to a mental hospital and his paternal grandfather founded a home for children with learning difficulties. However, the psychiatry professor had been what Jung politely described as 'not exactly stimulating'⁴ and psychiatry was held in some contempt by the medical profession of the time. This was an era before the discovery of any of the drugs that can help alleviate psychiatric illness and before the development of psychotherapy. Psychiatric hospitals were still lunatic asylums where the insane were locked away and forgotten in what were sometimes little more than prisons. As soon as Jung started to read his psychiatry textbook, he was hooked. At last in psychiatry, the medical treatment of mental illness, and in psychology, the study of the mind, there was a field of study which looked at the realm which most fascinated Jung, the inner realm. This was the realm of the unconscious and of dream and vision; the realm where realities collide. Psychiatry could bridge the gap between the scientist and the mystic in Jung.

Jung graduated with a good medical degree and was offered a prestigious post by one of his professors. To the university's consternation, he turned it down in favour of the lowly-paid profession of psychiatry. On 10 December 1900, Jung took up his first psychiatric post – as First Assistant Physician at the famous Burghölzi Psychiatric Clinic in the wooded outskirts of Zürich. The Burghölzi Clinic was the leading psychiatric hospital of its time. Under the famous psychiatrist Dr Eugen Bleuler, the Clinic tried out new methods such as hypnotherapy and dream analysis and its doctors read the pioneering works of Sigmund Freud.

Jung's working life was beginning. So too were other phases of his life. Just over two years into his career he married. Jung's first meeting with his future wife, Emma Rauschenbach, had occurred when she was fourteen. The Rauschenbachs were family friends of the Jungs. In 1902, when Emma was twenty, they met again. Jung went into hot pursuit. Emma turned

8   down his first proposal, but Jung persisted. Not long afterwards, on 14 February 1903, he and Emma were married. They
spent their honeymoon at Lake Como and then on a cruise to
Madeira and the Canary Islands. They could afford such luxu-
ries because Emma was the daughter of a successful industrial-
ist and independently wealthy. The financial future of the Jungs
was secure, but due to Jung's work, the young couple moved
not into their own house, but into a flat in the hospital. The first
of five children, Agathe, was born on 26 December 1904. Four
other children followed: Anna on 8 February 1906, Franz on 28
November 1908, Marianne on 20 September 1910, and Emma
on 19 March 1914.

In 1905, after just over four years at the hospital, in addition
to his medical duties, Jung was appointed to the prestigious
post of Lecturer in Psychiatry at the University of Zürich. As is
still the custom today, students were trained by having patients
brought into the lecture hall for the professor to examine and
make his pronouncements. One day a middle-aged woman on
crutches was brought in who was suffering from a painful
paralysis of the left leg. No physical cause being found, she had
been referred to the psychiatric department as a case of 'hysterical paralysis'. The patient did seem hysterical. Jung gave
her a chair and asked her to talk to his students about her illness. She went on and on and on. Desperate to silence her, Jung
interrupted and suggested that he try hypnosis to see if this
would help her. Before he could begin, the woman fell into a
deep trance from which she would not wake. Eventually she
came to, cried out, 'I am cured,' threw away her crutches and
walked out. Jung had performed his first miracle cure.
Embarrassed, Jung did not like to admit that he had not had
time to get around to hypnotizing her. 'Now you've seen what
can be done with hypnosis!' he told his students. In fact, he had
no idea what had happened, nor did his patient, but she was

deeply grateful. She went around Zürich proclaiming Jung a
miracle worker. Besides his work at the Burghölzi Clinic, Jung's
private practice began to grow.

JUNG AND FREUD

Meanwhile, in Vienna, Sigmund Freud, who was by then 49,
had been developing his revolutionary new treatment of mental illness, a form of psychotherapy known as psychoanalysis.
Freud had discovered that much of our behaviour was influenced by the unconscious mind. A fundamental assumption in
Freud's work was that we are seldom aware of the true causes
of our feelings and actions. These are largely unconscious and
hidden. Psychiatric illness was often caused by hidden conflicts
which, in Freud's view, originated in childhood sexual trauma.
Our unconscious contains material which we unable to accept
in our waking state. The answers to our problems lay within. If
patients could receive skilful help in uncovering the root cause
of psychiatric illness, they could deal with it. This was a new
way of dealing with the mentally ill and it fitted in with the
approach which Eugen Bleuler was developing at the
Burghölzi Clinic. The patient was treated with respect. Patients
were sources of potential knowledge about their illnesses,
rather than 'lunatics' who had to be locked up for their own
good. The role of the doctor was to ask the right questions, to
listen, to diagnose and to help patients help themselves.

Jung first learned of Sigmund Freud in 1900 when Freud's
famous book *The Interpretation of Dreams* was published. When
Jung first read the book he got little out of it, but three years
later, with his experience on the psychiatric wards behind him,
he returned to it. Jung found that Freud's explanation offered
the best rationale he had yet found for the mechanism of *repression*. Repressed memories are those that are too painful to face

and are thrust below the surface of consciousness. They emerge again in dreams and also when patients undergo therapy.

Freud's and Jung's backgrounds were both similar and different. Both were medical men from middle-class families. Both were fascinated by the life of the mind and had abandoned more lucrative aspects of medicine for the then 'fringe' specialism of psychiatry. However, Freud described himself 'an atheist Jew' who believed religion and the esoteric interests that were dear to Jung's heart were illusions. Jung was, if not an orthodox Christian, an earnest spiritual seeker. On his part, Jung could not go along wholeheartedly with everything Freud wrote. He did not believe that the cause of repression was always sexual trauma. He had observed that his patients repressed memories from trauma of all kinds.

In 1906, Jung decided to make contact with Freud. To introduce himself, he sent Freud some of his academic papers on word association, a technique he was using at the Burghölzi Clinic. In word association, the patient is given a string of different words and is asked to say the first word that comes into his or her head. From the responses given and the time taken to give them, the skilled therapist can identify unusual patterns of thought that indicate where in the past the source of trauma might lie. A similar process is used in the lie detector test, except that direct measurement is made of physiological responses to certain words or questions.

Freud wrote a gracious reply in response to Jung's papers, accompanied by an invitation to visit him in Vienna. As soon as he could get time off, Jung boarded train at Zürich and headed for Austria. He arrived at Freud's house in time for lunch and the two men talked non-stop for thirteen hours. Both men had found a colleague who shared their enthusiasms and their wish to do pioneering work in the realm of the mind.

Despite some reservations about one another's ideas, for the first two or three years the relationship flourished. Jung's father had died while he was still a medical student. Freud was about twenty years older than Jung, a major figure in the field where Jung wanted to make his mark, and Freud had no son. The visits between the two men became frequent and were supported by frequent correspondence.

Like Jung, Freud was preoccupied by religion, but mainly with the aim of freeing us from its delusions. In Freud's view, humans were motivated by two opposing biological instincts which he called by the Greek words *Eros*, meaning love and sexuality, and *Thanatos*, hate and aggression. The impulse to fertility and life competes within each of us with the urge for destruction and death. The most important instinct was Eros, and the primary component of Eros was sexuality.

Freud saw religious practices as rooted in the fears and wishes of childhood, especially in the *Oedipus Complex*. This is an important part of Freud's psychology. In ancient Greek myth, Prince Oedipus is abandoned as a child because it is foretold that he will grow up to kill his father the King. A shepherd family rescues the wailing infant who has been abandoned on a rock and adopts him. As a young man, Oedipus meets his parents without knowing their identity. Unwittingly, he kills his father in a quarrel and then marries his own mother, becoming king in his father's place. Freud believed that every young boy has a repressed rivalry with his father for his mother's affections. This 'Old Bull–Young Bull' tussle is something which must be resolved if the boy is to mature into a healthy adult.

Freud believed that religions, such as Judaism and Christianity, that worshipped Father Gods were worshipping nothing more than a projected father figure in the sky. God the father is a recreation of the omniscient and omnipotent father of infancy. The child is jealous of him, but fears him and must therefore appease him. Religious practices are a process of appeasing the 'Big Daddy'. Freud believed that religion could

12 play a purpose. Most people are insecure and unstable and need religious doctrines, rules of conduct and religious social support to maintain a stable life. However, in Freud's view, religion is essentially a crutch for the weak. The role of psychoanalysis is to free us from such delusions so that we can step boldly into a new and scientific world.

During the years of his friendship with Freud, Jung's conviction that there was a spiritual dimension within the human psyche was a source of friction. When Jung asked Freud his views on the paranormal, he replied, 'Sheer nonsense!' This upset Jung who felt a curious sensation in his diaphragm. It became hard and felt as though it was burning. At that moment, a loud crack came from the bookcase which stood next to the two men and they jumped in alarm. Jung told Freud it was an example of paranormal phenomena. Freud said this was rubbish. Jung retorted that soon there would be another manifestation. A second loud crack was heard. After this, Freud began to mistrust Jung. He felt that Jung had somehow acted against him.

Jung was impressed by what Freud had to say about the sex drive and recognized its importance, but he could not see sexuality as the be all and end all. When he spoke about his reservations, Freud explained that they were due to Jung's inexperience. At first, Jung went along with this, but as his psychiatric experience at the Burghölzi increased and his private patients grew, so too did the doubts. He could see that Freud was totally convinced by his 'sexual theory' but he became increasingly uncertain whether the theory derived from scientific observations or from Freud's own obsessions.

Jung was tremendously important for Freud. Until this point, most of Freud's followers were Jewish. The Jews were a minority in German-speaking society who experienced considerable prejudice and discrimination. If psychoanalysis was to flourish, it must become known within the mainstream medical community. For Freud, Jung was the ideal standard bearer. He was intelligent, creative, young, energetic, non-Jewish, cultivated and charismatic. In 1909, Freud made the father–son relationship more explicit. Freud informed Jung that he was adopting him 'as an eldest son, anointing him successor and crown prince' of his psychoanalytic movement. This should have been the crowning moment in Freud and Jung's relationship, but even as he was proclaiming Jung his successor, Freud was aware that Jung did not share all his views. Equally, it was apparent to Jung that Freud would never accept him having his own viewpoint; especially about certain matters that were dearest to Jung's heart – the spiritual realm.

In 1909, both men received an important invitation that marked a new development in psychoanalysis. Professor G. Stanley Hall, the 'founding father' of psychology of religion in the United States, invited them to lecture at the famous Clark University conference to celebrate the University's twentieth anniversary. Stanley Hall was the founding editor of the *American Journal of Psychology* and an enthusiastic admirer of Freud who was beginning to be recognized as an eminent figure.

This was not the era of the aeroplane. To reach America meant an eight-day crossing by ship across the frequently stormy North Atlantic ocean. Freud and Jung embarked at the port of Bremen in northern Germany. Even at the port, the tensions between the two men were becoming apparent. Freud had a sudden fainting fit and claimed that it was because Jung had a death wish against him. Freud interpreted every tussle Jung had with his ideas as a working out of the Oedipus Complex. It was never Freud's ideas that were wrong, but Jung's interpretations and psychological resistances. Jung was in a 'no win' situation. If Freud had suspicions against him, it was Jung's fault – a son's rebellion against his father. It was not so much

'Old Bull–Young Bull' as Old Bull–Young Lion: Freud the Taurus vs. Jung the Leo. Eventually something would have to give.

To pass time on the voyage, Freud and Jung analyzed one another's dreams. This was a serious mistake. There was too much suppressed conflict between the two men to go about this honestly. To Jung, some of Freud's dreams seem to involve a strong attraction Freud had to his wife's sister. Freud refused to discuss these dreams with Jung saying that it would undermine his authority to do so. This was the beginning of the end as far as Jung was concerned. By now, he was looking not for a father–son relationship, but for a meeting of equals. Jung could not accept Freud's stance and perhaps was too independent-minded ever to have been content for long with the role of disciple.

The visit to the States was a great success and probably took Freud and Jung's minds off the tricky subject of their relationship for a while. They were warmly received by the academic and medical communities, and their lectures received wide reporting in the press, even though they both lectured in a foreign language – German. Both men were awarded honorary doctorates of law at the conference. Off the lecture platform, they also had some entertainment. The distinguished Harvard professor William James brought along a medium whose paranormal manifestations had been thought impressive. In a short time, Jung and Freud between them managed to extract from her an admission that she was not clairvoyant at all but simply pretending in order to attract a young man. They also managed to do some travelling, visiting Niagara Falls and the Adirondack Mountains. The Clark conference was a major step in psychoanalysis being accepted into the English-speaking world. Freud's hope that psychoanalysis would become a world-wide movement was beginning to take shape. It was the first of a number of visits Jung would make to the States. He enjoyed the transatlantic crossings by liner, refusing always to travel by plane. He retained a permanent fascination with, but not always approval of, American culture.

On their return home, Freud continued to see Jung as his 'heir', chief apostle and propagator of the word; despite strong reservations expressed by Freud's other followers. They seemed to see much more clearly the conflict between the two men. In 1910, Freud insisted on appointing Jung Permanent President of the International Psychoanalytic Society and asked him to promise 'never to abandon the sexual theory. That is the most essential thing of all. You see, we must make a dogma out of it, an unshakeable bulwark.'[5] Jung asked him, 'A bulwark against what?' and was told that sexual theory would be a bulwark against the 'black tide of mud' which was occultism. What Freud meant by 'occultism' was everything dear to Jung's heart – philosophy, religion and mysticism. It seemed to Jung that Freud had lost his scientific objectivity and was descending into ideology.

BEYOND PSYCHOANALYSIS TO A SPIRITUAL PSYCHOLOGY

The final break between Freud and Jung came with Jung's publication of his book *Psychology of the Unconscious* which was later revised and called *Symbols of Transformation*.[6] This was published in two parts in 1911 and 1912. The *Psychology of the Unconscious* was an astonishingly broad-sweeping book that set out to examine the mythology of all major civilizations. Jung wrote the book at top speed in a poetic frenzy. Egyptian, Babylonian, Hindu, Classical, Gnostic, Germanic and Native American materials were incorporated. For Jung, myth was now the key to understanding the human psyche. He was no longer interested in individual psychology so much as the psyche of the whole human race – its dreams, myths and visions, and the religions and spiritual traditions that express them.

For Jung, myth was essential to the human race. To live without a myth which explains the cosmos, our place in it and how we are to live our lives was to be 'uprooted'. Without myth we would have no link to past or present. To understand ourselves we needed to understand the myths that had formed our civilizations. Individual consciousness was only 'the flower and the fruit of a season, sprung from the perennial rhizome beneath the earth; and it would find itself in better accord with the truth if it took the existence of the rhizome into its calculations. For the root matter is the mother of all things.'[7]

Through studying myth, Jung discovered that similar mythological patterns occur across cultures widely separated in time and space. He began formulating an idea radical to medical science at the time: that of a human group mind, the collective unconscious. This was a shift from a psychology which saw each individual's psyche as made up solely of his or her own past history to a vision of humankind as having a 'group mind' which was the inheritance of all. In this new psychology there was a role for spirituality.

To say the least, Freud reacted badly to the book. He saw it as a slap in the face; a complete rejection of all that he had taught his 'adopted son and heir'. Jung had rejected his theories and must pay the price. Jung suffered a profound psychological crisis. He had gone out on a limb in publishing his own theories and now suffered public rejection by his former mentor and colleagues. He was scared. Swiss society was and is conformist. To be part of a community was terribly important. To further his psychoanalytic work, he had given up his post at the Burghölzi Clinic. In 1914 he also resigned from his university post at the University of Zürich. Partly this was due to dissatisfaction because after eight years the university had failed to promote him to professor. Another important reason was that his mind was no longer focused on medicine but on the things of the spirit. For three years he could scarcely read a scientific book. Whether he willed it or not, something was turning him inwards to the world of the unconscious. He had been a leading figure in the psychoanalytic community and part of the academic establishment. Now he was alone and an outcast. Jung wrote:

> When I parted from Freud, I knew that I was plunging into the unknown. Beyond Freud, after all, I knew nothing; but I had taken the step into darkness.[8]

NOTES

1 Carl G Jung, *Memories, Dreams and Reflections*, recorded and edited by Aniela Jaffé and trans by R and C Winston, Fontana Paperback, 1995 ed, page 65.

2 Frieda Fordham (1966 ed) *An Introduction to Jung's Psychology*, Pelican, page 123.

3 *Memories, Dreams and Reflections*, page 72.

4 *Memories, Dreams and Reflections*, page 129.

5 *Memories, Dreams and Reflections*, page 173.

6 Carl G Jung, *The Collected Works of CG Jung*, Vol 5, *Symbols of Transformation*, Routledge & Kegan Paul, London, 2nd ed 1967.

7 Carl G Jung, *The Portable Jung*, Joseph Campbell ed, RFC Hull trans, Penguin, New York, 1976 ed, page xxi.

8 *Memories, Dreams and Reflections*, page 225.

A MAP OF THE PSYCHE

U nfortunately, there can be no doubt that man is, on the whole, less good than he imagines himself or wants to be. Everyone carries a Shadow, and the less it is embodied in the individual's conscious life, the blacker and denser it is.[1]

Now that Jung had broken from Freud, albeit unwillingly, he was free to pursue and develop his own ideas about the psyche. The word *psyche* is Greek and literally means mind; but Jung used it to include our behaviour, attitudes, feelings and ideas. The psyche is influenced by what is in conscious awareness and by what is not.

For Jung, life was a sacred quest and a journey. Life had meaning and purpose and it was his gift of conveying the meaning, purpose and beauty of life and consciousness to others that has made him so revered. If life is a journey, then we need a map to guide us. We also need a goal. The goal was self-discovery, the unveiling of who and what we really are. To help us, from his work with his patients Jung began to develop a new map of the psyche, a map that at the time was unique, though aspects of it have now been taken up by others.

For Jung, the human being was many-layered and many-faceted. Part of the process of self-discovery is a stripping away of the layers of the personality that prevent us seeing and being what we truly are. Jung wrote that as the layers of the personality are stripped away:

> In this way there arises a consciousness which is no longer imprisoned in the petty, over sensitive, personal world of the Ego, but participates freely in the wider world of objective interests. The widened consciousness is no longer that touchy, egotistical bundle of personal wishes, fears, hopes, and ambitions which always has to be compensated or corrected by unconscious counter-tendencies; instead it is a function of relationship to the world of objects bringing the individual into absolute, binding, and indissoluble communion with the world at large.[2]

The inner journey was not then a selfish one, but one which, by freeing us from the barriers which prevent us developing our abilities to the full, will at the same time allow us to use those abilities more constructively for others and so for society at large. Jung's message is an optimistic one. He believed that within each one of us was a centre of being, the Self, that is whole and true. For those whose lives and personalities have been damaged, this is a message of hope.

PERSONA

The first layer of ourselves is what Jung called the *Persona*. This is a Greek word which means 'mask'. The Persona is what we pretend to be. It is how we present ourselves to others. In part the Persona is designed to tell others something about ourselves. By the way we dress, speak and act, we create a particular impression. We 'stage manage' our performance and others will react to this. The Persona also fulfils the function of all masks. It is designed to hide from others those aspects of ourselves which we do not want people to see. These are the qualities of which we are ashamed. The Persona is an artificial personality. It is a compromise between our real identity and society's expectations, between our real identity and what we are willing to tell. Unfortunately sometimes people start to believe their own propaganda. We may act the part of perfect mother, daughter, doctor, receptionist, spiritual seeker, wise being, until we forget that this is only a role we have decided to play. Once people distinguish between who they appear to be and who they are, the process of self-realization can begin.

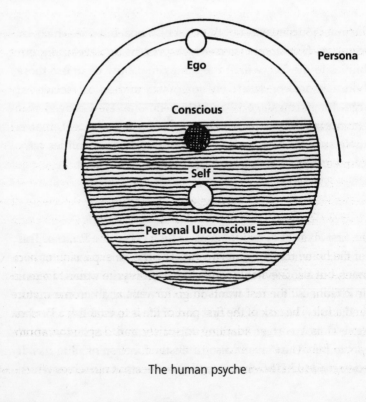

The human psyche

Another important aspect of ourselves is the *Ego*, a Latin word meaning 'I'. When thinking about the Ego, it is important to remember that Jung wrote originally in German where the term used was *das ich*. Written always with a small 'i', *das ich* means simply 'I'. It has none of the suggestions of Ego, egotism, egocentricity, that are found in the English language.

The Ego is who we think we are, as opposed to the *Persona* which is who we pretend to be. For most people Ego and Persona are different. We are aware that we are not the 'cleaned up' version of ourselves that we present to the world. Many of us will have friends and family with whom we can let the mask slip; let it all hang out. Away from the office, factory, hospital, school, or whatever, we can be who we are. If we become identified with the Persona, if we convince ourselves that the part we play is really us, then we become distorted. Other people are often aware of the distortion, even when the image is perfect. We meet saintly do-gooders who think of nothing but others, and our antennae tell us something is wrong. We feel uncomfortable in their presence and do our best to avoid them. Here we sense that they are playing a part, even if we cannot catch them at it.

In infancy the Ego develops. Children develop a sense of 'I'-ness – a sense of who they are and the social group they belong to. In puberty, the child moves out of the protective atmosphere of the home into the outer world. There is an expansion of horizons, but also inevitable conflicts. Part of psyche wants to remain in childhood; the rest wants to go forward and become mature and adult. The task of the first part of life is to establish a Persona (mask) as a way of adapting to society and displaying appropriate behaviour at different times and occasions. The healthy personality has the flexibility to take the mask off and on.

The Persona and Ego are within the conscious mind. Human beings are like icebergs. The conscious mind is only a small part of ourselves. There is much more underneath in the unconscious.

THE UNCONSCIOUS

Jung saw human consciousness as a remarkable phenomenon which had struggled into a precarious existence. Consciousness is nature becoming aware of itself – the capacity to know that we live and experience, the capacity to know that there is someone called 'I'. For human beings, the triumph of consciousness is not fully assured. In sleep, mental illness, mass movements, war, this can be overcome. It can also be overcome deliberately in religious ritual and in certain occult practices, such as mediumship, channelling, invocation of deities into priests and priestesses, and trance possession by deities as in the African-derived religions of *Santeria* and *Umbanda*.

Jung believed the unconscious had two levels: the *personal unconscious* and a deeper level called the *collective unconscious*. In the personal unconscious are those thoughts and feelings which we have repressed, suppressed or simply not noticed. *Repression* involves a more or less deliberate withdrawal of attention from thoughts, feelings or memories, so that normally we are no longer able to recall them. However, they may make themselves known to us through dreams, or in other states when the conscious mind lets go its grip on the unconscious, such as hypnosis. *Suppression* is sometimes confused with repression. Suppression is when we ignore something and thrust it out of consciousness so we can concentrate on something else. An example might be grief. If someone close to us dies, we might have to suppress the emotion we feel in order to go back to work and deal with our everyday life. Once home behind closed doors we can allow ourselves to feel our grief once more. In other words, we can access thoughts, feelings and memories that we have suppressed, but not those we have repressed. We also have thoughts, feelings and impressions that are fleeting and too weak to impinge on our conscious mind. However, they do register at a deeper level and are stored in the unconscious. These are known as *subliminal perceptions*. They may be retrieved under special conditions such as hypnosis.

SHADOW

Buried within the personal unconscious are important aspects of ourselves. The first of these which we encounter if we go on the spiritual quest is the *Shadow*. Often we think we know ourselves very well. Unfortunately the human mind is skilled at self-deception. Most of us are not what we think we are (the Ego), let alone what we pretend to be (the Persona). Our Ego is made up of those parts of ourselves which we can accept. We push into the unconscious those aspects of ourselves which we dislike, or which do not match our self-image. This part of ourselves is the *Shadow*.

Jung was a great believer in the human power of self-transformation but he also believed that the human capacity for aggressive, selfish and anti-social activity was infinite. Unfortunately, we are well aware of the potential in others for evil, but we fail to have true insight into our own negative nature and the extent to which our actions are corrupted by impulses to selfishness, jealousy, competitiveness and all the other evils of the human heart. For Jung, the key to change was acceptance of the Shadow – our own unacknowledged impulses. The less aware we are of our Shadow, the stronger it will be. We all know of hypocrites who mouth their support of worthy causes, whether spiritual, environmental or social, but who are spiteful and unpleasant people. Convinced of their own virtue, they denigrate others and may perform acts of violence and hate in the name of their ideal.

Not everything that we refuse to acknowledge about ourselves is bad and many qualities which are negative when repressed can become positive when given a proper outlet. Society and parental influence may teach us that certain qualities are undesirable when in fact they are not. Anger is an emotion that is frequently hidden, especially by women. While on the surface we may appear placid and loving, if this surface veneer is based on suppressing our own unhappiness, there may be a very angry Shadow within. A depressed person may be someone who has repressed his or her anger. Depression makes us flat, listless and lacking in energy. We may need to experience and come to terms with our anger in order to release energy into the psyche. Another problem with women suppressing their anger is that this can encourage women to accept treatment at the hands of men and from society which is totally wrong. If a woman suppresses her natural emotion in these circumstances, then her anger can turn inwards to a bitterness against herself; a force that can lead to suicide, abusive relationships, addiction and other self-destructiveness. Acknowledging one's own anger at injustice need not lead to aggression. Once we realize our own anger we can transform it; for anger is fiery energy. This energy can be channelled into creativity of thought and action and into changing the situation in which we find ourselves.

PROJECTION

One of the laws of the psyche is that repressed energy must go somewhere. If we refuse to acknowledge our own negative impulses and do not 'own' them, we will project them onto others. This happens on an individual level and on a group level. There are always individuals who we cannot stand, even though our friends think they are wonderful. It is like cat meets dog; the hairs on the back of our necks rise instinctively when we meet them. In Hermann Hesse's novel *Demian*, which was influenced by Jung's psychology, the great writer explained the projection of the Shadow.

> When we hate someone we are hating something that is within ourselves, in his image. We are never stirred up by something which does not already exist within us.[3]

The Shadow can also be projected onto other groups; particularly racial groups. Other races are frequently seen as inferior and as embodying all the worst characteristics of our own societies. Jews, Gypsies and ethnic minorities are groups which have been and are still victims of the projection of the Shadow. In Christianity, this split between bad and good is made explicit in teaching about God and the Devil. One is all goodness; the other all evil. The Devil can be seen as the Shadow of God.

In certain situations of great social stress, such as war, the Shadow can take over. We become possessed by demonic energy and the forces of hate, but believe this is righteous wrath and just anger. Possessed by our own negativity, we kill and torture one another and learn to hate other races, nations, and those whose religion and politics do not match our own. This can also happen on an individual level: the serial killer who, by killing women, prostitutes, homosexuals, or whoever, believes he (and it is usually he) is cleansing society of evil. This is a type of madness.

When first we seek to know more about ourselves, whether through therapy or through any spiritual system that encourages us to look inwards, we are likely to encounter the Shadow.

In other words, we are going to find out that we are much nastier people than we would have ourselves believe. This is a difficult step to take but, as Jung would say, it has the virtue of honesty. We are taking a courageous step and looking at ourselves in the mirror of truth. We may not like all that we see there, but we can be comforted by the fact that at least we are facing our own darkness while others are not.

ANIMA AND ANIMUS

Once we have confronted the Shadow, the next step on the journey is to uncover other hidden aspects of ourselves. Here we come to an idea which seems quite commonplace now, but which was much more radical in Jung's own time. No one is wholly male or wholly female. We all contain an aspect of ourselves which is our 'contra-sexual' side. In a woman, this male side of herself is called the *Animus*. In a man, his female side is the *Anima*.

The Anima/us is related to the Persona. As men or women we create a Persona that incorporates what our societies teach us is appropriate male or female behaviour. In the West, this used to mean that men were forbidden to cry and women were forbidden to be strong and independent. The Anima/us compensates for this. It is the part of ourselves that contains characteristics of the opposite sex which we do not normally publicly express. The more sexually stereotyped our upbringing, the greater will be the difference between the Anima/us and our everyday personality.

ANIMA

The *Anima* is the archetypal image of womanhood present in the unconscious of every man. Jung believed that it develops from three sources: a man's mother, his experiences of women as companions, and his own femininity which is grounded in the female sex hormones found to some extent in every male body. The Anima often appears in dreams.

If a man is unconscious of his own inner feminine, he will project this onto women in his life; at first his mother, and then his female partners. While a man is unconscious of his Anima, his love relationships will be disastrous. He will fall in love again and again; only to be disappointed. After a time, his beautiful goddesses will be discovered to be real women – with personalities of their own. Until he breaks the cycle, he is likely to keep moving on to the next woman who seems a close enough match to receive his Anima projection. Many film stars and media personalities have owed their success to being unobtainable goddess figures who could carry the Anima projections of their male fans. Marilyn Monroe, Evita and Diana, Princess of Wales, all had this quality. The more a man tries to be masculine and to suppress his own inner feminine, the more he will be at the mercy of the projected Anima. Violent and unstable men who project their Anima onto a woman will perceive the chosen woman to be part of themselves. This can lead to intense obsessive love which in the extreme can lead a man to kill the woman if she tries to leave him. Alternatively, violence may turn inward. A man may commit suicide because he is unable to live without what he perceives to be part of himself rather than another human being.

ANIMUS

The *Animus* is a woman's inner masculine. The word is Latin and means 'spirit'. Jung wrote much on the Anima and relatively little on the Animus, a symptom of the fact that he could not understand it as well as the Anima. It was Emma Jung who developed the concept of the Animus.[4] She saw the Animus as symbolizing for women four major qualities: Word, Power,

Meaning and Deed. Typically, Animus figures appear wise, strong, competent and adventurous – the qualities of stereotyped masculinity. Women can fall in love with their own Animus projected onto a seemingly suitable male, just as men can fall in love with an Anima projection. It will seem that this male figure will come and sweep us off our feet like fairytale princesses and henceforth take care of us, relieving us from all the boring, mundane cares of the world, such as earning our livings. Romantic fiction of the Barbara Cartland variety thrives on this type of fantasy. To turn to another literary *genre*, Ian Fleming's character James Bond is an archetypal Animus figure – clever, handsome, skilled, brave and a marvellous lover. Any relationship based on Animus projection will collapse under the weight of the demands for the man to be all perfect. The Anima usually appears in dream as a single female figure. The Animus often appears in plural. The Animus often makes its presence felt in the constellation of characters of the spiritualist medium. Female mediums rarely have female spirit guides. They are usually one or more males who appear in the guide of Wise Old Men, such as a Native American chief, Tibetan master or doctor.

PERSONALITY TYPES

In 1913, Jung began to have a series of terrible visions of Europe bathed in blood which seemed to him later to foretell the outbreak of the First World War. In July 1914, Jung was invited to Britain to lecture to the annual conference of the British Medical Association in Aberdeen in northern Scotland. He was there when war broke out and had to make a series of difficult train journeys through the Netherlands and Germany to get home to Switzerland. The war seemed a horror and a collective madness. In Germany, the outbreak of war was greeted with insane euphoria. Shopkeepers were giving away food and not bothering to take payment; so happy were they to be launching themselves into war. This brought home to Jung the power of the forces of the unconscious to arise and overwhelm civilization. Whole nations were in the grip of their Shadows.

Switzerland was neutral in both the First and Second World Wars, but its people were still affected by the war, albeit not so greatly as those in other parts of Europe. Food was short and the army was on alert in case any country should decided to ignore Switzerland's neutrality and attack. Swiss men were called up for army service and everyone at home was subject to food shortages. Jung was called up for several months at a time. Initially, he worked as a medical doctor, treating the complaints common to an army on 'stand by' – corns, bunions, coughs, colds, stomach aches and syphilis. His abilities were recognized however and by 1917, he was put in charge of an internment camp. According to the Geneva Convention, any military personnel from the German or Allied sides who escaped into Switzerland had to be interned for the duration of the war. Jung's camp, the Chateaux d'Oex, was for British prisoners. Conditions for war time were relatively pleasant. The British government paid for wives to come to Switzerland to be with their husbands and officers could live in hotels or *pensions* in the town. The main problems were boredom and frustration. Jung found himself dealing with the psychological malaise of those who were trapped in a situation where they had nothing to do and where their former comrades were still fighting on the front while they were cocooned in safety. Jung arranged for officers to attend university courses in neighbouring cities and did all he could to improve day-to-day living conditions and stop outbreaks of disease. This contact with British prisoners confirmed in him a strong liking for the British. Jung had already visited Britain more than once. His first trip had been in 1904 when he took two months leave from the Burghölzi Clinic and went to London to improve his English. Jung liked what he saw as the rugged individualism of the English which contrasted with Swiss conformity. After the War Jung made many trips to Britain which were influential in strengthening Jungian psychology in Britain. These included visits to major cities and to the Dorset and Cornish countryside. In Cornwall, he was impressed by the Atlantic coast, the dark cliffs, the lashing sea and the standing stones.

When not called up, Carl Jung spent much of the First World War exploring the spiritual history of Europe in order to understand what he saw as the deep identity crisis which had caused the War. This resulted in the publication of Volume 6 of his *Collected Works*, *Psychological Types*.[5] The first part of *Psychological Types* is a history of personality theory from the ancient Greeks onwards. In the last part he develops his own theory. Jung's theories about personality are one of the aspects of his work that people are most likely to encounter in their everyday lives. His typology has been used to develop the Myers-Briggs Type Indicator®, a personality questionnaire widely used in careers guidance, counselling, management development and team building.

Jung believed there were four basic personality types and then various sub-divisions resulting from interaction between them. The four types operated differently in the world and were characterized by four different modes of being which Jung called the *four functions*. Jung divided the four functions into two groups – *perception* and *judgement*. *Perception* tells us what is happening. It is the process by which we receive information. The two perceptual functions are *sensation* and *intuition*. *Judgement* makes decisions about what to do with the information gleaned by perception. Our judgmental functions are *thinking* and *feeling*.

Sensation operates through the physical senses – our eyes, ears, etc. It is the means by which we discover facts. Intuition shows us meanings and relationships that are beyond the reach of the senses. Sensation is grounded in the present. It tells us what is happening now. Intuition looks beyond the present and tells us how situations are likely to develop in the future. Intuition is the function of the imagination – telling us how things might be. Sensation is the function of factual memory – telling us how things are and used to be.

Thinking tells us whether something is logical and rational. We need our thinking function when dealing with machines. Feeling is equally important. It tells us what is valuable, worthy and good. We need our feeling function when dealing with people. Thinking without feeling is detached, cold and cruel. It applies the letter of the law without taking account of individual circumstance. Feeling without thinking is partisan. People are seen as more important than rules. It will favour those it likes and ignore those it does not. It will adopt ideas because it admires the person who teaches them rather than because they seem meaningful and true.

Thinking and feeling judge situations in different ways. If we are good at thinking, we are likely to be less good at feeling and *vice versa*. Sensation and intuition perceive different aspects of situations. If we begin to perceive and process the sensate aspects of a situation – the detail – we are less likely to be able to use our intuition to perceive the overall picture.

The example in Figure 2 leads with Thinking. This person's thinking is his or her most developed function. He or she will be good at work that deals with machines, systems and things. Computer specialists need a well-developed thinking function. The thinking person will tell us things that are true, but they may also be tactless and cruel. The thinking person lacks empathy and does not realize how his or her words can hurt because

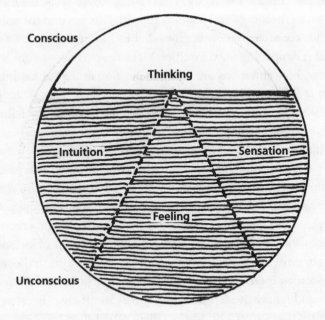

The four functions with Thinking dominant

the opposite function of feeling is hidden in the unconscious and does not work very well. The person will be unaware of his or her feelings. However, when they do reach the surface, the thinking person can be swamped by them. The other two functions, sensation and intuition, are on the borderline between consciousness and the unconscious. As the person develops, they will become more accessible and easier to utilize.

If the functions are reversed, we would have a dominant feeling function. This is the situation where someone is good with people, sensitive to what is going on, good at becoming

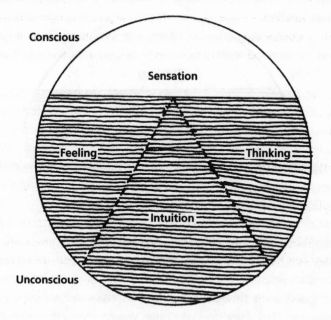

The four functions with Sensation dominant

involved; but thinking is less developed. The feeling person will lack the detached, rational and possibly 'cold' approach of the thinking-dominated person.

The feeling-dominated person can become fanatical and may find it difficult to judge the quality of ideas. We can see the feeling function at work in the media, politics and religion. Causes are espoused with irrational enthusiasm and without stopping to judge and evaluate them properly to decide if they are true. A plausible and charismatic leader who arouses people's feelings can sell them ideas and policies that are seriously faulty.

Hitler engaged the feeling function of millions who worshipped him as a god. Thousands killed themselves in despair when he died.

In Figure 3, the dominant function is Sensation. The person is likely to be good with things and facts, and at home with his or her body.

The sensate person is likely to be practical and observant. Intuition is in the unconscious and he or she will distrust anything which is non-tangible. Spirituality, dreams, visions, religion, may be dismissed and called rubbish if there is no material proof of them. Sensation-function people love crafts, cooking, gardening, historical research, archaeology; anything that can be seen, heard, tasted, touched or smelt.

If the functions were reversed, intuition would appear as the dominant function. Intuitives are creative and imaginative. They are full of ideas; but start much more than they finish. They are interested in the new rather than the old. Intuition is not good with things and facts. Intuitives are so busy day dreaming that they do not notice where they are going and bump into lamp posts. They are good at lateral thinking, creative ideas and 'seeing round corners', but do not notice what is in front of their faces. The intuitive will not be at home with the practical and is bored by the nitty-gritty. Intuition sees situations in terms of the whole rather than the detail.

Jung believed that as we grew and developed, so too would our personalities. As children our lives are dominated by one of the functions, so that our personalities are very one-pointed. As we approach teen age, a second function emerges and we become more multi-faceted and multi-skilled as we gain conscious access to new parts of ourselves. In adulthood a third function should emerge, usually around middle-age. The function which emerges will be that closest to the threshold between consciousness and the unconscious. New interests may develop as the third function emerges and our lives may spin off in other directions. Many people never reach this stage and remain fixed in their adolescent personalities; sometimes because they refuse to acknowledge the changes that are struggling to take place within them. They may try to thrust an emerging function back into the unconscious. Others go further and access their fourth function, the one that is most elusive. To be balanced and to create the perfected Self, we must learn to use all four functions.

> For complete orientation all four functions should contribute equally: thinking should facilitate cognition and judgement, feeling should tell us how and to what extent a thing is important or unimportant for us, sensation should convey concrete reality to us through seeing, hearing, tasting, etc, and intuition should enable us to divine the hidden possibilities in the background, since these too belong to the complete picture of a given situation.[6]

This does not mean that we will all use all four functions equally and all emerge with the same personalities. We will continue to be true to our dominant type, be it feeling, sensation, intuition or thinking, but we will be able to use the other functions when appropriate. The fourth function is always the function that is opposite our dominant function. If we are sensation types, our intuition will be the last aspect of ourselves to appear. If we are thinking types, then our feeling response, our ability to relate to others, will be the last aspect of ourselves that we master.

In families there is a tendency to share out pressures and expectations. There may be pressure to make a child fit a preconceived pattern. For example, a feeling child in a thinking family might be pressured to be more thinking. We can do this, we can play a role, but we will not be authentic. Eventually we will have to break out and become ourselves if we are to develop and grow and avoid psychological disorder. In relationships we may find that we have to take on the activities of one of the functions, even if they are not naturally 'us'. When my partner was less sensate than I was, I had to look after all the bill paying and the banking. Now I am married to someone who, while not sensate, is more so than I, I am relieved to leave all that detail to him.

EXTRAVERSION AND INTROVERSION

In addition to the four functions, another influence on how we behave is a dimension that interacts with these. This is *extraversion* (spelt with an 'a' in Jungian psychology) and *introversion*. Extraverts and introverts differ in two fundamental ways. One aspect is impulsiveness. When we meet a new person or situation, the extraverts amongst us say, 'Yes!' The introverts are more inclined to say, 'No!' Extraverts jump in with both feet and find themselves in a mess. Introverts say 'Yes' more slowly, but from a saner place. They are more likely to stick with a decision once they have made it, but they may miss out on opportunities. Timing is critical in this. Introverts need time. The extravert is more immediate. If we are working with people, training them or dealing with them in a therapeutic situation, it is important to know that introverts take longer to take new ideas on board. School favours the extravert. 'Who knows the answer? Hands up!' is the teacher's cry. Extraverts are happy to put their hands up regardless of whether they are sure they are right or not. Introverts know the answer but do not put up their hands in case the answer is wrong.

A second aspect of introversion–extraversion is sociability. The stereotype of the introvert is someone who hates going to parties. It is true that extraverts love parties as opportunities to network and meet new people and that extreme introverts hate going to parties, but few people are extreme introverts. Introverts like going to parties, providing they know some of the people. A room full of strangers is both boring and intimidating to the introvert. Introverts love parties where they know everyone. They enjoy giving their own parties – providing the guest list is carefully vetted. Introverts are not anti-social but a difference between introverts and extraverts is that introverts also need time on their own. Extraverts do not. An extravert will happily flat share with ten other people. This is paradise for an extravert because there is always someone at home to talk to. Extraverts need an audience and someone to listen to them. Their ideas are formulated by talking them through with others. Introverts gestate their ideas on their own, e.g. in libraries; extraverts develop them through debate over a drink in the student bar.

SELF

The term *Self* is *'das Selbst'* in German and conveys the idea of the essence of something. As with all translation, finding equivalent terms in different languages is difficult. 'Das Selbst' in German is more impersonal than 'Self' in English. It suggests more of a separation from who we think of as 'I' ordinarily than does the English word. The term was derived by Jung from Hindu thought and the idea of *Atman* – the divine Self within. Jung turned to the East because he could find no Western term which could convey the depth of the idea of the Self. The Self was not soul or spirit, but something both wider and deeper – the totality of a human individual. In Hinduism, *Brahma* is the unknowable, infinite, transcendent Creator of the Universe. *Atman* is the divine within; the totality and centre of finite human existence which can be experienced. Hindus are taught that 'Brahman is Atman and Atman is Brahman'. In other words, at the core of our being is a divine spark that is part of the greater whole which is the divine energy of the universe. *Brahma-Atman* includes all opposites, all ambiguities of life, good and evil, light and dark. The Self is the sum total of all the psyche, both conscious and unconscious. It represents the integration of all the disparate parts of ourselves – Persona, Ego, Anima/us and Shadow, and the four personality functions. In accepting all the different aspects that make up our personality, we become who and what we really are.

Images of the inner divine Self, the whole and perfect being that our psyche would like us to become, are deep within each one of us. The Self may appear to us in the form of a Wise Old Woman or Man, but often the image appears in dreams and fantasy not as something human but as some sacred and holy object – the Grail, the Sun, the pearl in the lotus, the philosopher's stone, the hidden treasure. These are all images which have appeared in the myths of different cultures as Self; the treasure hard to attain which we must go on a spiritual quest to find. The Self is the place from where our image of the divine is born and the source of our spiritual longing.

There is no connection in early life between Self and Ego. As children and adolescents, our first task is to form a Persona that can deal with the world, and the true Self is unknown. This is appropriate when we are trying to find our place in the world. We need to find a way to function and effectively deal with the everyday demands of reality. However, if that situation continues permanently, we become arid and our lives 'dry up'. We need the 'moisture' of the unconscious if our lives are to be rich and whole.

The unconscious is often symbolized in myth and dream by water such as the sea. Our bodies are largely made up of water. Our psyches are largely made up of the unconscious. To access the greater part of ourselves we have to go down into the depths

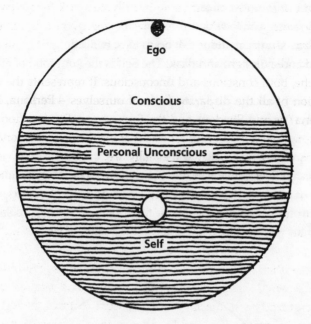

The psyche with no connection between Ego and Self

of the waters of the unconscious to bring back to the surface of consciousness the deepest part of ourselves – the Self.

It is difficult to describe the Self. It is an inner experience and as such is beyond words. The language of poetry can sometimes convey it, or the language of image. Here is a description from a Hindu sacred scripture, the *Brihadaranyaka Upanishad*:

> As a man in the arms of his beloved
> is not aware of what is without and what is within,
> so a person in union with the Self

is not aware of what is without and what is within;
for in that unitive state,
all desires find their perfect fulfilment.
There is no other desire that needs to be fulfilled,
and one goes beyond sorrow.[7]

Another description of the Self comes from a Hindu Jungian analyst. It is:

> ... pure awareness, light and illumination, the fulfilment of one's destiny. It is not the state of unconsciousness of a stone or matter. ... It is not a metaphysical concept or a hypothesis of science, but a matter of experience, supported by all the mystics and prophets of the world ... the end and aim of the journey of life.[8]

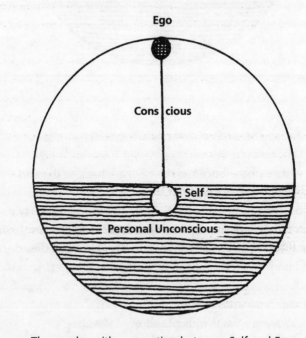

The psyche with connection between Self and Ego

For Jung, the Self represented the fullest potential of the human psyche and, unlike Freud, he saw the Self and not the Ego as the ruling force in the psyche. The Self was both personal and transpersonal. It emerges from the hinterland between two different levels of the unconscious – the personal unconscious and the collective unconscious. The collective unconscious was one of Jung's most important ideas. From this source came the possibility of transformation.

NOTES

1 Carl G Jung, *Collected Works*, Vol 11, *Psychology and Religion: West and East*, Routledge & Kegan Paul, London, 2nd ed 1968, page 131.

2 Carl G Jung, 'The Relations between the Ego and the Unconscious' (1928) in *The Collected Works of CG Jung* Vol 7, *Two Essays on Analytical Psychology*, Routledge & Kegan Paul, London, 2nd ed 1966, page 275.

3 Hermann Hesse, *Demian*, WJ Strachan trans, Panther Books, London, 1969, page 106.

4 Emma Jung, *Animus and Anima: Two Essays*, Spring Publications, Zürich, 1957, page 20.

5 Carl G Jung, *The Collected Works of CG Jung*, Vol 6, *Psychology Types*, Routledge & Kegan Paul, London, 2nd ed 1971.

6 *Psychological Types*, page 518, para 900.

7 Eknath Easwaran, trans *The Upanishads*, Arkana, London, 1988 ed, chapter IV, verse 19–21, page 45.

8 J Marvin Spiegelman and Arwind U Vasaveda, *Hinduism and Jungian Psychology*, Falcon Press, Los Angeles and Phoenix, 1987, page 157.

THE MAGIC OF TRANSFORMATION

We should never identify ourselves with reason, for man is not and never will be a creature of reason alone, a fact to be noted by all pedantic culture-mongers. The irrational cannot be and must not be extirpated. The gods cannot and will not die.[1]

Jung completed his doctoral dissertation in 1902, two years after beginning work at the Burghölzi Clinic. The research was on mediumship and Jung's cousin and her seances formed a substantial part of it. Even in these early days, the themes were beginning to emerge that were to form the basis of Jung's work. Jung argued that the unconscious is intuitive and is more receptive than the conscious mind. It carries memories lost to consciousness and contains knowledge of which we are not consciously aware. During sleep walking and in mediumship, or what we today would call channelling, autonomous, independent personalities can take control of the psyche. These are the medium's 'spirit guides'. These may be aspects of the medium's own personality, or they could be independent entities, but either way, if the psyche is fragile, these other voices can take over the personality and lead to illness. Another interesting idea that Jung was beginning to formulate was an optimistic one for the psychologically afflicted. He believed that psychological disturbance has purpose. It can show us the way out of dilemma and trauma. A final idea was that within the human psyche are patterning forces which may in different individuals at different times and places produce the same spontaneous 'constellations of fantasy'. It was these 'constellations of fantasy' that evolved into Jung's idea of the archetypes.

THE COLLECTIVE UNCONSCIOUS AND ARCHETYPES

The material within the personal unconscious is based on our own personal experience. It is derived from past events that have happened to us individually. Deeper within the unconscious are layers formed not in the personal life of the individual, but during the millennia the human race has existed. This is the *collective unconscious*. The collective unconscious is an immense warehouse, a collective and inherited memory, and a depository for the sum total of human knowledge to date. This is our psychic inheritance.

Jung's vision was not of human beings as purely biological animals, as in the work of Darwin or Freud, but of humans as spiritual beings. Freud preferred the term *subconscious* for the unconscious and to him it represented something inferior to the conscious mind. It was dominated by animal instinct rather than human rationality and was a kind of psychic dumping ground. It was a trash can for all the aspects of ourselves that we have forgotten or do not wish to acknowledge; usually because society tells us they are immoral or unworthy. For Freud, the subconscious was concerned solely with the past. For Jung, the unconscious was also concerned with the future. The unconscious was in the process of creating new ideas which in time would emerge into our conscious awareness. However, there was a more fundamental difference between Freud's and Jung's ideas of the unconscious. For Jung, the unconscious contained not only personal material but also material that transcended the personal and came from the collective psyche of humankind. For Jung, then, we were not isolated in our individuality. Humans were individual and unique, yes; but also inter-related and interconnected in the deepest part of ourselves. The unconscious was the realm of the archetypes, a word which derives from the Greek – *arch*, origin, and *tupos*, imprint. These are the forces which cause spiritual transformation.

After the publication of *Symbols of Transformation* in 1911–12, in which he developed some of the ideas outlined in his dissertation, Jung was rejected by the psychoanalytical community whose Freudian gospel he had questioned. Only a few friends and his family stood by him and he was thrown into trauma. He was beset by strange dreams and fantasies. Some non-psychologist biographers have claimed that he was verging on schizophrenia. This was not the case, but he was plunged into a severe psychological and spiritual crisis. There were two ways forward. He could try and suppress his visions, or he could face them, record them, analyze them and incorporate them into his psychological theories. He did the latter. Jung's own spiritual quest could be said to have begun in earnest with his rejection by the Freudian community. Jung was thrown back on his own resources. In December 1913, he started to explore the material that his unconscious was revealing to him. He began an intense exploration of his already active dream life. He also explored his fantasies and waking dreams using a visualization exercise. This was to evolve into the technique of *active imagination* which is widely used in Jungian analysis. Jung visualized that he was digging down into the earth and entering underground galleries and caverns where he encountered archetypal figures. He would enter into dialogue with the figures, asking them who they were and what they sought. In this way he could communicate with the disparate parts of his psyche and uncover their meaning. This type of technique will be familiar to those used to visualization and pathworking.

As he recorded this material, Jung became aware that two levels of dreams, images and visions were emerging from his unconscious. Some related to his own personal life and past. Other material was different. Its themes were mythological, archetypal, spiritual and religious. Many of us will be aware from our own dream life that some dreams are based on the events of the day. Often these dreams bring to our attention aspects of situations and emotions that we have not consciously noticed. Other dreams are 'big dreams'. Often these are very vivid. We know they have powerful symbolic significance for us, even if we do not immediately understand their meaning. These are concerned not so much with the past but with the present and future. Somehow they tell us where we are going.

Jung began to check the images that appeared from these 'deeper' dreams with those of his own patients, and with the themes and images found in the world's myths. This reinforced his early ideas about the spontaneous 'constellations of fantasy' which become the archetypes and myths that are the bedrock of human myth and culture. The archetypes were an innate readiness to reproduce the same mythical ideas in all cultures and at all periods of history.

> One could almost say that if all the world's traditions were cut off
> at a single blow, the whole mythology and the whole history of
> religion would start all over again with the next generation.[2]

Jung saw the archetypal images from the collective unconscious as the building blocks of religion. It was from these that our images of the gods and their myths are created. These are

46   the seeds which, planted in the soil of different times and cultures, develop into separate flowering plants. Their common inheritance is apparent to those who study them, but the shape they take on varies according to the climate in which they find themselves. Jung observed that myths and fairytales contain certain symbols or motifs that are also found in daydreams, visions, dreams and delusions. They have a 'numinous' or fascinating and magical quality that engages the psyche, whether we like it or not.

The different aspects of the personality that I described in the previous chapter – the Self, Anima, Animus and Shadow – are some of the many 'primordial images' or archetypes that arise in the psyche from the collective unconscious. These images are found in the cultures of all historical periods; albeit in different dress. Sometimes the archetype of the Self appears in the psyche as a person – a Wise Old Person or a Sun Child. Both appear because both old age and childhood take us nearer the realm of the unconscious, in which is hidden the Self.

Other archetypes cannot be depicted by the psyche as 'persons' but come in the form of more abstract archetypes of transformation. The archetypes of transformation symbolize typical situations, places, ways and means by which illumination comes. The Self can also appear in abstract form as an archetype of transformation. These transformational images are known in both Western and Eastern esoteric traditions. The pictures that accompany the transformation stages of alchemy are an example; as are some of the major arcana of the tarot, the chakras in Yoga and Tantra, and the ox-herding pictures of Zen.

We may think of the tarot as primarily a means of divination. However, like many such systems from the esoteric traditions, its images are thought to reflect not only the mundane events of our everyday lives, but also deeper psycho-spiritual processes occurring within us. In the tarot, it is the minor arcana, the equivalent of the suits in playing cards, that relates more to the everyday world. In esoteric tradition, the major arcana, the tarot trumps, are thought to depict the archetypal forces that are at work in any given situation. Western esoteric traditions have well-developed systems for meditating on the tarot. These are similar to Jung's psychological technique of active imagination.

The major arcana of the tarot contains archetypes which are both personal and transformational. Sallie Nichols, who trained with Jung in Zürich, describes the archetypal journey of the tarot in her book *Jung and the Tarot*.[3] She describes the first seven of the major arcana from the Magus to the Chariot as the Realm of the Gods. The last seven images from the Devil to the World represent the Realm of Illumination and Self-Realization. The middle seven cards from Justice to Temperance, all cards concerned with equilibrium in different forms, represent the Realm of Earthly Reality and Ego Consciousness.

The middle cards are the mediators between the Realm of the Gods and the Realm of Self-Realization. In other words, they represent us being acted on by the archetypal forces of the Gods above. The last seven cards represent the results of this process. These are seven different states of illumination. The Fool stands outside all this: he is both beginning and ending, manifestation and dissolution. The tarot archetypes contain manifold meaning. They are ambiguous and can never be finally pinned down. We can return to them time after time and find fresh understanding within them.

INDIVIDUATION

The journey to attain the Self and to become who and what we really are was called, by Jung, *individuation*. He regarded individuation as the central concept of his psychology and an important contribution to the study of religion and psychology.

The Prediction Tarot

The archetypes represent the different encounters and stages of the individuation process. They are the beings we must meet and processes we must undergo on our personal journey of self-realization. For Jung, individuation was the summation of all his thought and work. The journey is a difficult one and requires courage. First we must let go of the Persona, the protective mask. Then we must face our own inner darkness. We must withdraw from others those aspects of ourselves that we have projected onto them and we must be willing to see both ourselves and them as we really are. This can disrupt our relationships. We may find that we are not the people we thought we were; nor are they. The relationships and activities that satisfied us in the past are no longer appropriate on the next stage of our journey. This can be painful and difficult to face. Sometimes we may find that we have lived our lives wrongly; that we have to go back and start again.

The process of individuation that Jung lived through and which he observed in others involves an activation of the arche-types and entering into dialogue with them. This process can be precipitated by sincere immersion in a spiritual tradition. It is also the goal of Jungian psychotherapy. However, the process is not without its dangers. Wise teachers have always warned about the perils of setting out on the path unguided and ill-prepared. Although we are dealing with what might seem mere images, Jung warned that these were extremely powerful forces and not to be meddled with lightly. The esoteric traditions of the East and in the West, both Christian monastic traditions and the Western Magical Tradition, warn of the glamour that sur-rounds the world of the imagination. The archetypes can prove fascinating, so fascinating that we may identify with them and allow them to take over our personality. If a handsome man sees us as the epitome of his Anima – the wise, all-powerful, allur-ing and beautiful Goddess of his dreams – it can be very tempt-ing to play the part assigned to us. For a while, we may be successful but gradually our own personality will leak out and the result will be disillusionment and bitterness on both sides. The same trap can occur in other relationships. If we are in authority positions where others project on to us wisdom, authority and greatness, we can easily find ourselves falling into the trap of putting on the mantle that others have prepared for us. It is easy for politicians to succumb to their own propa-ganda and to believe that they really are the wise beings that their spin doctors have created. In the extreme, this leads to psychosis. The archetype takes over the personality and we are no longer in the driving seat.

Jung's concept of individuation is not to be confused with individualism. We do not seek individuation just for our own sakes, but to better contribute to society. Jung believed that the challenge for human beings was to become whole. Only through growth and integration will we find meaning and fulfilment. Failure to meet this challenge will bring neurosis or psychosis and, if unconsciousness is widespread in society, discord and destruction.

Jung's psychology was very positive about the second half of life. Freud was concerned with freeing us from the traumas of childhood in order to help us cope with the everyday world. Jung was less interested in childhood and more concerned with adult life. Jung's own life began to open up in middle age and onwards. He began to travel more widely outside Europe. In 1920 when he was about 45, Jung visited Tunisia and Algeria in North Africa. Orderly Switzerland is the land of watch and clock makers. What struck Jung immediately was that in the North African Arab culture people did not live by clock time. Theirs was a different rhythm of life with different priorities – something which he found very attractive.

In 1924 and 1925 he visited another non-clock watching people, the Native Americans of Taos Pueblo in New Mexico. For the pueblo inhabitants, the divine was immanent or in-dwelling in nature. The sun, the local mountains and the waters were sacred. Another and perhaps the most significant journey for Jung occurred in 1926 when he went south into Africa to Mount Elgon in Kenya and the sources of the Nile. Africa had an enormous impact upon him and he felt that his return trip down the Nile to Egypt became a drama of the birth of the light.

Jung's experiences of non-Western culture were highly formative. They helped him see beyond the European mind set and showed him that there were other ways of living and perceiving. These trips also influenced Jung's spiritual ideas. Jung saw the way of life and belief systems of these non-European peoples as being valid and important. When in Taos, he made friends with a Native American chief who was governor of a pueblo. His friend talked to him about the 'white man', saying:

> We don't understand the whites; they are always wanting something – always restless – always looking for something. What is it? We don't know. We can't understand them. They have such sharp noses, such thin, cruel lips, such lines in their faces. We think they are all crazy.

Jung commented that, 'My friend had recognized, without being able to name it, the Aryan bird of prey with his insatiable lust to lord it in every land – even those that concern him not at all.'[4] Jung saw it as Western megalomania to assume that Christianity was the only truth, and the 'white Christ' the only Redeemer. He came to believe that the export of Western religion was a form of European cultural imperialism which subverted other people's belief systems and cultures, with extremely negative effects. The West had introduced the opium trade to China and enforced monogamy brought large-scale prostitution and sexually transmitted diseases to Africa. 'And the good European pays his missionaries for these edifying achievements!' commented Jung in mystification.

In the early 1920s when he was approaching 50, Jung had started to build a stone tower at Bollingen on Lake Zürich on land that had belonged formerly to a monastery. Jung had been inspired by the traditional way of life he had found outside Europe and wished to create a retreat where he could live as simply and as close to nature as possible. There was no electricity or gas at Bollingen. Oil and wood stoves were used for heating and cooking and lamps for light. At first, water had to be filtered from the lake, but later Jung brought in a water diviner who found a spring. The Tower could be reached only by boat or by a half-hour walk from the railway station. Bollingen became his rural retreat where he could most truly be himself. Here he chopped wood, cooked, wrote, painted and took up stone carving. Perhaps more importantly, the quiet and seclusion of Bollingen allowed him to focus on his inner life and on his writing.

At Bollingen, he had time and space to develop the ideas that would become the focus of the second half of his life. Jung saw life as having two distinct phases, both of which are about learning. The first half is characterized by expansion of the personality and adaptation to the outer world. We go out into the world and make our way. We study, gain qualifications, get jobs, become parents. This is the extraverted phase of impacting on the outer world. The second half is characterized by a turning inward to the inner life. The transition between the two phases is the mid-life crisis. This is often a time of difficulty. The demands of life are different in the two phases and the rules change. Jung believed it was a problem of Western culture, and the United States in particular, that the focus was totally on what should be the tasks of the first half of life – worldly success. People tried to stay young and rejected the inner journey necessary for the second half of life.

Jung believed that in the first half of life, introverts may feel they have missed out. They will be more at home with the task of second part of life – the inner journey. In the second half of life, extraverts may feel that they have 'dried up' inside. If we have focused on external things and external success, we are faced at mid-life with the problem that others are challenging our position and are coming up from behind to outstrip us. If we judge ourselves purely by our impact on the outer world and our powers are beginning to weaken, what else is left?

In the mystical and spiritual traditions, the inner experience of individuation has always been seen as the most valuable and important thing in life; the only thing that can bring lasting satisfaction. The external trappings and baubles – power, glory, wealth – are transient and futile. Some of Jung's patients were extremely rich and, as his fame grew, those from millionaire families such as the Rockefellers would fly from the United States to Europe to see him. Jung found that whereas by all worldly standards rich people should be happy, often they were not. They were 'bored to death'.[5] Only spiritual realities could sustain us.

It was during the years of the First World War, when he was 39 to 44, that Jung's own spiritual crisis reached its climax; but what about those whose spiritual quest begins much younger in life? Jung was wary of those who began the spiritual journey before they had dealt with the outer world and some of the early issues and problems of personal development. There is no doubt that spirituality can be a refuge and an escape from reality. This is the danger of some New Religious Movements which demand communal living and submission to a religious leader or guru. This can be an abdication of the difficult responsibility of becoming adult.

For Jung, religion was about spirituality. He was not interested in the social functions of religion. For him, all the religions of the world had arisen in order to help us solve the problem of finding the Self, the divine within, and of unifying ourselves with it. Orthodox religion could be both a hindrance and a help in the spiritual quest. Jung pointed out that one of the Latin roots of the word religion was *religare* – rejoining. He saw the Ego's awareness of the reality of the Self and of the inner world and its efforts to reconnect or rejoin with the Self as the essence of religion. This indicates that religion is an inner activity. Jung was an introvert and attracted by the Eastern way of thinking which emphasizes that self-liberation and enlightenment can be achieved by personal effort alone. Jung believed that a danger of Western religions was that they taught that what we perceive as 'God' or 'the Gods' exists outside ourselves. The emphasis is on a movement outward towards an external and transcendent personal God, rather than inwards towards divine consciousness. In the outer forms of Christianity, it is through the grace of an external God, which may or may not be given, that salvation comes. We are dependent on the outer rather than the inner.

Jung's own spiritual quest began in his childhood Christianity, but in the austere and respectable world of the Swiss Reformed Church, no spiritual ecstasies were found, no mystic vision. To find what he sought, Jung had to go elsewhere.

ASTROLOGY

Jung's interest in the paranormal had already brought him to the fringes of the occult. The study of myths inspired his ideas of the collective unconscious and stimulated his interest in Pagan antiquity and in those less-known schools of Western thought which in the Christian era had secretly guarded and nurtured the Pagan mysteries. Jung also become interested in astrology. By 1911, he had trained himself to interpret natal charts. During the period 1906–1913, Jung wrote frequently to his mentor Sigmund Freud and it is in these letters that we find reference to his astrological researches. On 8 May 1911, Jung wrote to 'Dear Professor Freud':

> At the moment I am looking into astrology, which seems indispensable for a proper understanding of mythology. There are strange and wondrous things in these lands of darkness.[6]

This was during the period that he was writing *Symbols of Transformation*, the book that was to cause the final rift between the two men. Jung was concerned about how Freud would react to his dabbling in astrology and went on to write:

> Please don't worry about my wanderings in these infinitudes. I shall return laden with rich booty for our knowledge of the human psyche. For a while longer I must intoxicate myself on magic perfumes in order to fathom the secrets that lie hidden in the abysses of the unconscious.[7]

Presumably Freud's response was not too forbidding, for on 12 June 1911, Jung wrote again to Freud that his evenings were largely taken up with astrology. His natal charts had shown him some remarkable insights into their subjects' personalities. He had also found that he could predict aspects of the personalities of their parents from their charts.

Although it was never a major focus of his work, astrology was an important stepping stone for Jung. It emphasized for him the correlation between the inner and outer worlds, and between events in the wider cosmos and events within the individual psyche. Jung's interest in astrology continued throughout his life, but he was a great debunker of newspaper horoscopes. He was unconvinced by the influence of the Sun sign; despite being in many ways an archetypal Leo male. Jung believed it was the season in which we are born, rather than the zodiac sign, which influences the personality. However, he was interested in the effects of planets on the personality; for instance, the 'Mars effect' which has been researched more recently by French scientist Michel Gauquelin and described in scientific papers and in his book *Cosmic Clocks*.[8] Jung was also interested in the precession of the equinoxes. The astrological sign in which Spring occurs moves slowly backwards through one degree of longitude every 72 years. This means that every 2,000 years, the sign of the zodiac on the horizon at spring equinox moves back one. In the Northern Hemisphere at present we are leaving the Age of Pisces and entering the Age of Aquarius. This means, of course, that people who think of themselves as Ariens are now Aquarians—which makes conventional astrology somewhat confusing! Jung believed that the precession of the equinoxes was of important historical and spiritual significance. Each change of era would herald in a new spiritual tradition. The Piscean era from 0000 CE to around the end of the twentieth century was the era of Christianity. Jung thought it significant that the fish symbol was widespread in early Christianity and was used as a secret sign amongst Christians during eras of persecution. Phrases such as Christ being the 'fisher of men' occur frequently in the *New Testament*. In recent years, fundamentalist Christians frequently display fish symbols on their cars; an unconscious recognition perhaps of their adherence to the outgoing Piscean Age and its values.

If we are influenced by the cosmic movements of the planets and the zodiac, this suggests the reality of the ancient occult maxim: As above, so below. This was to become an important theme in Jung's work.

GNOSTICISM

Jung often referred to his journey into the unconscious during the years immediately before and during the First World War as his *Nekyia* or 'Night Sea Journey'. The term comes from the classical Greek myth of Odysseus. Odysseus was required to serve on the side of the Greeks in their war against the city of Troy. Troy lies in what is now Asian Turkey. This was the war precipitated, so legend tells us, by the elopement of the beautiful

Helen who left her Greek husband Menelaus to run away with her Trojan lover Paris. Menelaus raised a Greek expedition to bring back Helen. The Greeks laid siege to Troy for ten years before the city fell. It took Odysseus and his companions a further ten years of adventuring to return home. Odysseus' journey took him through magical encounters with the sorceress Circe, who turned his men into pigs, and battles with mythological figures such as the one-eyed giant Cyclops. Odysseus' many adventures still provide the stuff of television series and Hollywood films today. One adventure was a journey into the Underworld, the realm of the dead. It is this that is called the *Nekyia*, the Night Sea Journey.

During his *Nekyia*, Jung had a number of significant 'big' dreams, whose meanings took him years to unravel. One of the first was in December 1912 when he dreamt that he was high up on the magnificent wide open balcony of the tower of an Italian castle. The balcony had pillars, a marble floor and a marble balustrade. He was seated on a Renaissance chair made of gold looking out into the distance. In front of him was a beautiful table made of emerald. His children were seated around the table. Suddenly a white dove-like bird descended. When it landed it transformed into a beautiful little girl with blonde hair. She ran away to play with his children but then came back and threw her arms around him. Then suddenly she vanished and transformed into a dove once more. The dove spoke and told Jung, 'Only in the first hours of the night can I transform myself into a human being, while the male dove is busy with the twelve dead.'

Jung could not decipher the dream, but he knew that it was important. In Christian symbolism the dove is the Holy Spirit, the third person of the Christian tri-partite deity. Jung wondered whether the twelve could be the twelve apostles of Christ. If so, what was the dream telling him? Here we can see clues as to where his spiritual life was going. Jung believed that the emerald table signified the Emerald Tablet of Hermes Trismegistos, a legendary magician who figures in mythology of the Western Magical Tradition. It was the translation of the magical works of Hermes Trismegistos into contemporary European languages that stimulated the revival of the magical tradition in fifteenth-century Renaissance Europe. On the Emerald Tablet are engraved the words, 'As above, so below'. In other words, whatever happens in the microcosm of our own psyche is mirrored in the outer world of the macrocosm, and vice versa. This saying became the motto of the Renaissance magicians and of those mysterious magicians-scientists, the alchemists. In Jung's dream, the male dove, the Holy Spirit of Christianity, was preoccupied with twelve dead men who belonged to the past. Jung's future lay in reconnecting with another past, the past of the Renaissance and in hearing the voice not of the male dove but of the female. The symbol of the female dove was found not in Christianity but in another faith which had rivalled Christianity in its infancy – Gnosticism. Here the female dove is Sophia, Divine Wisdom.

Many of us are familiar with the term *Gnostic* but who and what were the Gnostics? *Gnosis* is a Greek word which means knowledge. The Gnostic movement began just before the Christian era – around the fourth century BCE. The Macedonian Greek general Alexander the Great had conquered many of the civilizations of the Near and Middle East – Egypt, Palestine, Syria, Babylon and Persia. The Greek settlers who followed Alexander's army included philosophers who began to combine Greek and Eastern thinking. In this new climate, as in more recent times, spiritual seekers went East to gain enlightenment by being initiated into the mysteries and brought back with them new ideas. Babylonian astrology, Greek Stoicism and Platonism, Judaism, the Egyptian mysteries and other Pagan mystery traditions, such as those of Mithras and Orpheus, began to mingle. This process was hastened by the Romans who captured much of the territory previously held by the Greeks and incorporated this into the Roman Empire.

Under the Romans, the urban world around the Mediterranean from Italy through Greece and into Turkey, Palestine, Lebanon, Egypt and north Africa was not so different from our modern Western world. Rome created a multicultural, multiracial, multi language and multi faith society open to new ideas. The spread of these ideas was accelerated by the movement of people. The Empire was full of people travelling to and fro at the service of armies, political masters or simply in pursuit of that most important of human drives – profit. Trade flourished and ships plied regular routes from port to port. Large cities were built with every modern convenience that the more limited technology could provide, from sewers to street lighting, to theatres, shopping precincts, brothels and universities. One million people lived in the sophisticated sacred city of Ephesus on the Turkish coast which was dedicated to the Goddess Artemis. This was the city from which the Christian missionary Saint Paul was ejected by irate silversmiths who believed his new God would damage their trade in Goddess images. There were also semi-universal languages. What English is today, so Greek and Latin were then. The educated of many races and nations could use these languages to communicate ideas and read each other's thoughts on parchment scrolls, papyrus sheets or wax tablets. Learning, ideas and religious innovation flourished. In this climate was born Gnosticism, a spiritual tradition that sought enlightenment within.

In Gnosticism, nature and material creation are viewed as fundamentally flawed and evil. Creation manifests through the actions of Sophia, the female personification of Wisdom, whose activity creates a movement in the *Pleroma*, the divine realm of light with its deity the True God. This creates a series of increasingly inferior emanations (rather like the ripples in a pool), until finally our universe, a realm of chaos, darkness and evil, comes into being. Our universe is ruled by seven *archons*, or in some versions the Prince of Archons, the *demiurge*. Ignorant of the true God, the archons rule the cosmos like a vast prison, enslaving humankind. At death the divine spark within each human being – the pneuma – should return to the divine realm, but the archons act to prevent this. The appetites and passions of the body and psyche conspire to bind the divine spark to the material realm.

Without redemption by the revelation of the truth, the saving knowledge or *Gnosis*, the divine spark or *pneuma* remains ignorant and in captivity. Gnosis brings knowledge of the true state of things and also knowledge of the transcendent God of the divine realm, who is otherwise unknown in this world. The mystical knowledge of salvation is brought from the realm of light by a saviour – *Primal Man*. Primal Man awakens the divine spark within us and teaches us the rites and knowledge necessary to help us find our way through the realms guarded by the archons to the divine realm. In this belief we find echoes of the *Egyptian Book of the Dead* and other mystical works written by the ancients to guide the soul through the Otherworld to the realm of the gods.

Jung believed that the Gnostic vision of the return of the divine spark within us to the divine realm was a symbol of the spiritual journey described in his process of individuation. Initially, we live in the chaotic realm of outer darkness at the mercy of the archetypes, symbolized by the seven archons. This state of consciousness is ruled over by the Ego, symbolized by the tyrannical demiurge. The Ego thinks it is the ruler of the psyche and does not realize that if the psyche is to evolve, it must relinquish its place to the Self, symbolized by Primal Man:

the greater, more comprehensive Man, that indescribable whole consisting of the sum of conscious and unconscious processes.[9]

Gnosticism was a serious threat to early Christianity. Some early Christians identified the blood-thirsty God of the *Old Testament* of the *Bible* with the demiurge. They distinguished him from the True God who sent Primal Man in the form of Jesus as a saviour to redeem the world through mystical knowledge. However, from the 4th century CE onwards, Gnosticism lost its impetus and its ideas were absorbed into other forms of mysticism and into the Western magical tradition. The Gnostic view of how the universe was created is similar to, though not identical with, that found in the Medieval Jewish mystical tradition of the qabalah. In qabalistic-based ritual magic, Gnostic doctrines that describe the ascent of the soul through the celestial spheres to divine union are transformed into ritual techniques to seek unity with the divine on the earthly plane.

Jung's interest in Gnosticism was not its relationship to the magical tradition, but its description of the transformation and spiritual purification process necessary to achieve unity with the divine. This he saw as a metaphor for the process of individuation, whereby we seek an inner unity, not with a transcendent God, but with the divine within – the Self. Jung saw the Gnostics as early spiritual psychologists. He took their doctrines as evidence that the psychological processes he saw in himself and his patients were known throughout the ages; though veiled in the language of mysticism and religion.

Other intimations began to emerge that the realms of the Gnostics and alchemists held keys to what Jung sought. Early in 1914, Jung had a dream in which a strange being appeared that he named 'Philemon'. Jung did not know his origin but felt that he was a Pagan and had emerged from the last years before the birth of Christ, the time of the Graeco-Egyptian Gnostic mysteries. Philemon's image was a strange mixture of human, animal and bird. He came as an old man with a lamed foot, the horns of a bull and the wings of a kingfisher. Similar composite images are found in alchemical texts. The kingfisher is often associated in mythology with Christ, but the horns spoke of other Gods. The lamed God is an image drawn from Pagan mythology and is found both in Greek and Germanic traditions. It is an image associated with shamanism and with the image of the wounded healer – an appropriate symbol for Jung at this time. Shortly afterwards Jung received what he saw as a sign that Philemon was important. Kingfishers were extremely rare in the area where he lived, but he found a dead kingfisher in the garden. Although dead, the bird was still beautiful and undamaged. Jung entered into interior dialogue with Philemon who became his inner teacher. Jung longed for a teacher of flesh and blood but no live guru was available to him. The unconscious helped him by providing him with Philemon. Jung wrote later in his autobiography:

> All my works, all my creative activity, has come from those initial
> fantasies and dreams which began in 1912, almost fifty years ago.
> Everything that I accomplished in later life was already con-
> tained in them, although at first only in the form of emotions and
> images.[10]

Jung's paranormal experiences from his teenage years and twenties continued throughout his life. In 1916, it seemed to Jung that his inner world was undergoing another change. Philemon wanted a 'voice'. A series of strange happenings occurred, and it seemed as though his house in Küsnacht was haunted. One Friday night, his eldest daughter Agathe who was eleven woke in alarm to see a ghostly white figure passing through her bedroom. That same night, his second daughter

Anna who was ten twice had her blanket snatched from her bed, and his eight-year old[11] son Franz had an anxiety-provoking dream. On the Saturday, Franz drew a picture of the dream in which appeared a fisherman, an angel and a devil. Everything culminated about five o'clock on the Sunday afternoon. The front door bell began ringing insistently. The maids looked out from the kitchen to see who was there but although they could see the bell moving, no one was pushing it. A strange thick atmosphere began to pervade the house until it seemed as though a crowd of spirits was present. Jung heard them cry out in a chorus, 'We have come back from Jerusalem where we found not what we sought.' The message was clear. The answer to Jung's spiritual quest was not to be found in the Holy City of Christianity. Immediately afterwards Jung began writing at top speed *Septem Sermones ad Mortuos*, 'Seven Sermons to the Dead', completing it in three evenings. Jung felt his writing was almost as an act of mediumship. He said later that he could not put his name to the work because it did not seem as though it was he who wrote it. Instead he attributed *Septem Sermones* to the famous heretical Gnostic Basilides of Alexandria (117–161 CE).

Seven Sermons to the Dead is a 'Book of the Dead' in which Jung advises the newly dead on how to find ultimate redemption. The dead are Crusader knights whom Christianity has failed. In the first six sermons we learn of an alternative religious viewpoint from Christianity and of Basilides' God who is named 'Abraxas'. In the seventh sermon, Jung reveals the secret: redemption or rebirth cannot be found outside ourselves and through the mediation of an external deity as in the Christian tradition. The answer is Pagan and is to be found by turning inwards to seek the inner sun, the God within. Subsequently Jung wrote two other books influenced by Gnosticism – the *Black Book* and the *Red Book*. Neither have ever been permitted to be published.

At the time Jung was writing, few Gnostic texts had been found and most knowledge of Gnosticism came from Christian opponents. Jung could see within Gnosticism useful parallels with his own thought. However, Jung began to find the study of Gnosticism dissatisfying. It seemed too remote and disconnected from his own time. There must be a bridge, something that connected his own ideas and those of the Gnostics – but what was it?

ALCHEMY

Alchemy was practised until the seventeenth century and beyond. It went into decline from 1661 with the publication of Robert Boyle's *The Sceptical Alchemist* which overturned Aristotle's four element theory. Jung first started reading about alchemy in 1917, but at that stage it seemed obscure and even rather silly. In 1926, his unconscious sent him a series of dreams that awakened his interest once more. The dreams involved a house that was situated beside his own house and had an annex. Jung dreamt that he went into the annex and discovered that it contained a wonderful library dating mainly from the sixteenth and seventeenth centuries. Inside some of the books were curious engravings and symbols. Later Jung realized these were alchemical symbols.

Grounded in the natural philosophy of the Middle Ages, alchemy formed a bridge on the one hand to the Gnostic past, and on the other into the future, to the modern psychology of the unconscious. The popular idea of alchemy is of an early form of chemistry that attempted to turn base metals such as lead into gold. Alongside this, alchemy had another purpose – the transformation of the practitioner. On the one hand, alchemy is the precursor to modern chemistry. On the other, it is a complicated synthesis of philosophical, mystical and religious ideas. The word itself is Arabic. Like Gnosticism, its origins lay in the convergence of Eastern and Western ideas that was the result of Alexander the Great's conquest of Egypt. Greek philosophy discovered the Egyptian religious and initiatory traditions and, just as importantly, Egyptian technology. The Egyptians were skilled metallurgists, fabric dyers and perfume makers; skills which involved chemical processes. The Greeks had philosophical theories about the nature of matter. Famous alchemists included Maria Prophetissa or Mary the Jewess, sister of Moses, Zosimos, Paracelsus, Albertus Magnus, Roger Bacon and John Dee. The legendary maxim of Maria Prophetissa:

> One becomes two,
> two becomes three,
> and out of the third comes the one as fourth.[12]

… was influential in helping Jung develop his idea of the four functions. First the personality would be dominated by one function, then a second would emerge, followed by a third which would be opposite to the second, and finally the fourth. This creates what is sometimes known as 'the Way of the Snake'.

Alchemy's exoteric goal – the transformation of base metals into gold – was logical given the theory of matter at the time. This was based on Aristotle's four element theory. Aristotle believed that the world consisted of *prima materia*, prime matter, that had only potential existence. To exist it needed form. Form in turn gave rise to the four elements of Air, Fire, Water and Earth in different proportions. If one could change the proportions of the elements, the nature of the substance would change. By working on the elemental composition of any substance, it could be turned into any other.

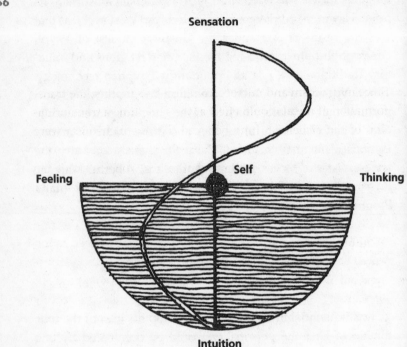

The Way of the Snake

Esoteric alchemy was interested in something different. Alchemy was not just an early scientific and technical process. It involved an elaborate cosmology in which the human being, the microcosm, was a reflection of the cosmos, the macrocosm. This philosophy was expounded on the Emerald Tablet of Hermes Trismegistos which featured in Jung's 1912 dream. He quotes in *The Psychology of Transference* a variation on the famous principle of Hermes Trismegistos found in the alchemical work of Athanasius Kirchner, *Oedipus Aegyptiacus*, published in Rome between 1652 and 1654:

Heaven above, Heaven below;
stars above, stars below;
all that is above, also is below.
Grasp this and rejoice![13]

Since macrocosm and microcosm reflect one another, the transformation of metals could effect at the same time a transformation of the alchemist. Jung believed that the alchemists were projecting onto matter their own psychic processes. Some were aware of the deeper symbolic meaning of their art, but the majority were not. Clues that alchemy was an analogy for inner transformation are found in the preparations made by the alchemists. Success was dependent on the practitioner's state of mind. This must be devout and pure. Prayer and meditation were necessary. The practitioner had to renounce all covetousness and 'lust for result' in order to proceed from an attitude of detachment and compassion. In the dreams of many of his patients who were going through the individuation process, Jung found images strongly resembling those of the different stages of Medieval alchemy. His friend the famous Swiss Jewish quantum physicist Wolfgang Pauli (1900–58) who helped him develop his ideas on synchronicity had similar dreams.[14] The stages of alchemy were a sophisticated symbol system representing the archetypes of the collective unconscious and the different stages of the individuation process.

What were these stages? There are three distinct stages of transformation. The first is the *nigredo* or blackness. Prime matter, the alchemists' original base substance, contains two substances – sulphur (male or sun) and mercury (female or moon). The alchemist pulverizes prime matter, mixes it with a secret fire, places it in a sealed vessel and heats it. This causes the prime matter to blacken and then to dissolve and decompose. This decomposition reveals the two complementary substances

CONIVNCTIO SIVE
Coitus.

The Sacred Marriage

of sulphur and mercury. Psychologically, Jung believed that *nigredo* represents a breaking down of the barriers between the conscious and unconscious mind. This can lead to 'blackening', a state of depression and melancholy. We are confronted with the Shadow, our own inner darkness; the process that Jung called his *Nekyia*, when everything seems desperate and lacking in meaning. This is known as the *Dark Night of the Soul* in Christian mysticism.

As the process continues, the separating out occurs. There is a dawning awareness of the opposite and conflicting tendencies in the psyche – the male and female within. In a man there is an encounter with the Anima; and in a woman an encounter with the Animus.

The second stage of the alchemical process is *albedo* or whiteness. In alchemy this is represented as the outcome of a series of processes requiring furnaces of varying temperatures and an elaborate array of stills, flasks, and other apparatus, including the alchemist's miraculous spherical vessel. The substance produced by the *nigredo* begins to show white flecks and turns white as it is washed clean. Finally the substance becomes volatile and crystallizes as a white stone. This is the stage when the psyche is cleansed. We face up to our inner darkness and hidden projections and take ownership of the disparate parts of ourselves. By confronting the archetypes and entering into dialogue with them, they come into awareness. This is the first goal. Through suffering the purgatorial fire of self-discovery, a unification becomes possible. The unconscious gradually becomes illuminated and the *albedo* stage is reached.

Rubedo or redness is the final goal. The white stone is added to mercury and 'exaltation' takes place. The stone turns green – symbolized in alchemy by the appearance of the Green Lion – and then turns red. In alchemical language, the opposites have united. The white queen has fused with the red king in the Sacred Marriage or *hieros gamos*. From this sacred marriage, a new being or substance is born and the king and queen die. This new being or substance is symbolized as the *elixir vitae* (elixir of life) that brings long life or even immortality. It can also be symbolized as philosophical gold or golden glass, a rose, a winged hermaphrodite representing unity of body, soul and spirit, or as the Philosopher's Stone, described by the Greek alchemist Zosimos as:

this Stone which is not a stone,
a precious thing which has no value,
a thing of many shapes which has no shapes,
this unknown which is known of all.[15]

For Jung, this final *rubedo* stage represents the balanced unification of the differentiated psyche, from which is born a new vantage point for the psyche, the ideal of wholeness which Jung calls the *Self*. The impact on Jung of the insights he gained from alchemy cannot be over-estimated. Alchemy had prepared the ground for understanding the unconscious, by leaving behind a template of the individuation process that was clearer than that found in the dreams of any single individual.

When he began his study of alchemy Jung had a dream in which he entered the courtyard of a seventeenth-century castle and found himself trapped when the gates clanged shut behind him. A voice said, 'Now we are caught in the seventeenth century.' On waking Jung felt resigned to this and his unconscious sent him the comforting thought, 'Someday, years from now, I shall get out again.'[16] Jung studied alchemy and was 'stuck in' the seventeenth century for a long period. He accumulated a library of alchemical books like the ones in his dream, but later he was 'released' and moved on to other things.

Alchemy and Gnosticism had brought Jung to a place where East meets West, but one of the triggers which helped him understand the texts of the Medieval alchemists was an ancient text written in another continent and another era. This was *The Secret of the Golden Flower*, a text of Chinese alchemy. On the one hand it provided for Jung the key to understanding Western magical traditions; on the other it began a twenty-year exploration of Taoism, Buddhism and Hinduism, the major traditions of the East.

NOTES

1 Carl G Jung, *Collected Works*, Vol 7, *Two Essays on Analytical Psychology*, Routledge & Kegan Paul, London, 2nd ed 1966, page 72.

2 Carl G Jung, *The Portable Jung*, Joseph Campbell ed, Penguin NY, 1976 ed, page xiii.

3 Sallie Nichols, *Jung and the Tarot*, Weiser, York Beach, Maine, 1980.

4 *Modern Man in Search of a Soul*, pages 246–7.

5 Carl G Jung, *Dream Seminars*, Vol 1, *Unpublished Works of CG Jung*, page 210, quoted in Marvin Spiegelman and Arwind U Vasavada, *Hinduism and Jungian Psychology*, 1987, page 23.

6 William McGuire, ed, *The Freud/Jung Letters: The Correspondence between Freud and CG Jung*, Ralph Manheim and RFC Hull trans, abridged by Alan McGlashan, Penguin Books, London, 1991 ed, page 223.

7 *The Freud/Jung Letters*, page 223.

8 Michel Gauquelin, *The Cosmic Clocks*, Granada Publishing Ltd, St Albans, 1973.

9 Carl G Jung, *The Collected Works of CG Jung*, Vol 9, Part 2, *Aion*, Routledge & Kegan Paul, London, 2nd ed 1968, page 189.

10 Carl G Jung, *Memories, Dreams and Reflections*, recorded and edited by Aniela Jaffé and trans by R and C Winston, Fontana Paperbacks, 1995 ed, page 217.

11 In his memoirs (*Memories, Dreams and Reflections*, page 215) Jung describes his son as nine years old when this occurred, but this seems to be a mistake.

12 Carl G Jung, 'Introduction to the Religious and Psychological Problems of Alchemy' (1944) in *The Collected Works of CG Jung*, Vol 12, *Psychology and Alchemy*, Routledge & Kegan Paul, London, 2nd ed 1970, para 26.

13 Carl G Jung, *The Collected Works of CG Jung*, Vol 16, *The Practice of Psychotherapy*, Routledge & Kegan Paul, London, 2nd ed 1966, page 189, para 384.

14 Carl G Jung, *The Collected Works of CG Jung*, Vol 18, *The Symbolic Life: Miscellaneous Writings*, Routledge & Kegan Paul, London, 1976, pages 284–5.

15 Carl G Jung, 'The Visions of Zosimos' (1954) in *The Collected Works of CG Jung*, Vol 13, *Alchemical Studies*, Routledge & Kegan Paul, London, 1967 edition.

16 *Memories, Dreams and Reflections*, page 228.

THE LIGHT OF THE EAST

My admiration for the great philosophers of the East is as genuine as my attitude towards their metaphysics is irreverent. I suspect them of being symbolical psychologists, to whom no greater wrong could be done than to take them literally.[1]

From the late-nineteenth century onwards, Eastern philosophy and religious ideas were becoming familiar to educated Europeans. Darwin's explanation of evolution and other scientific advances had undermined literal belief in Christianity. People were seeking new spiritual avenues. The Theosophical Society founded by Madame Blavatsky introduced a synthesis of Hinduism, Buddhism, Neoplatonism and Western esoteric thought into Europe. There was a growing interest in Eastern mysticism. Hindu and Buddhist sacred texts had been translated into European languages. In 1893 the World Parliament of Religions in the United States brought together religious leaders of most traditions and gave the East a higher profile amongst Western thinkers. From the late-nineteenth century onwards, it became possible for the educated Westerner to find out about Eastern spirituality without ever leaving his or her native city.

Jung's knowledge of Eastern religions began in childhood. While his father taught him Latin, sitting in their Protestant parsonage his mother read him stories of the Hindu deities. He found these stories endlessly fascinating. This interest continued into adulthood. By the time he wrote what became Volumes 5 and 6 of his *Collected Works*, *Symbols of Transformation* (1911–12) and *Psychological Types* (1921), he had gained an extensive knowledge of Hindu, Buddhist and Taoist thought.

The period that followed was the time of his *Nekyia* crisis. His rejection by the Freudian community was one cause. Another was problems in his marriage. Jung had married young and while he loved his wife Emma, initially at least she seems to have been a conventional Swiss housewife who could not help him develop his interests. He longed for an intellectual companion. At some point between 1913 and 1914, a former patient and trainee analyst Antonia (Toni) Wolff (1888–1953) entered his life and became his lover. It was she who introduced him to new aspects of Eastern philosophy and to astrology and helped him develop some of his most important ideas. Emma Jung, who seems to have been an heroic woman, decided to accept the situation. Toni Wolff became part of the Jung family circle until her death. She was usually a guest at the family Sunday lunch and frequently travelled to conferences and seminars with Jung while Emma looked after their children. Naturally, his wife found this difficult to accept, but early-twentieth-century Switzerland was not an era or country where today's solution, divorce, was common. People, especially women, accepted all types of relationships which today we would not. On Jung's part, despite his need for Toni Wolff, Jung never contemplated divorce and continued to love Emma.

MANDALAS

Towards the end of the First World War, a sign came that his psyche was beginning to integrate itself. Jung began drawing *mandalas*. He produced his first mandala in 1916 after writing his Gnostic 'Book of the Dead' *Septem Sermones*, but at that point he did not understand what it was. *Mandala* is a Sanskrit word and is a circular image which is drawn, painted, danced or enacted, in order to assist meditation. Usually the design has a centre and fourfold divisions involving designs such as multiple interlocking squares, stars, or double squares – octagons.

A mandala

Each day while commandant of the Chateaux d'Oex intern-ment camp, Jung drew a mandala which seemed to correspond to his psychological state. He found that creating these harmo-nious patterns of a circle with a central point helped overcome the imbalance in his psyche. He realized that the mandalas rep-resented the Self with the psyche unfolded around the centre. They were symbols of wholeness and integration, intimations of where his psyche was going. It is also significant that they were symbols from an Eastern tradition; for the next stage of Jung's psychological exploration lay in the East.

TAOISM

Was Tao the child of something else?
We cannot tell.
But, as a substanceless image,
it existed before the Ancestor.

There was something formless yet complete
that existed before Heaven and Earth;
without sound, without substance,
dependent on nothing,
unchanging, all-pervading, unfailing.
One may think of it as the Mother of all things under Heaven.
Its true name we do not know;
Tao is the name that we give it.[2]

Taoism (pronounced more like 'dow-ism') is the most ancient known system of Chinese spiritual philosophy. It may be over 5,000 years old. Taoism, Confucianism and forms of Buddhism were the main spiritual traditions of China before it became communist. Some aspects of Taoist tradition have become familiar to us through the introduction into the West of Chinese medical techniques such as acupuncture. These aim to rebalance *Yin* and *Yang* energy within the body.

The Taoist text the *Tao Te Ching* by the famous sage Lao Tsu has been translated into more languages than any book except the Christian Bible. Although Taoism is a philosophy, its interest is more in the development of intuitive wisdom than logical reasoning. Logical reasoning is seen as limited and incapable of understanding life's deeper mysteries. *Tao* is difficult to translate. Christians sometimes translate it as 'God', but this is misleading. 'The Way' is a common translation, but Jung preferred Richard Wilhelm's translation – 'meaning'. Jung also gives the alternatives of Heaven, principle, natural force, life force and prime cause.[3] The focus in Taoism is on living life in harmony with nature and the natural order of things. Taoism influenced Chinese and Japanese art which frequently depicts the human figures as small beings in a greater natural landscape. An appeal of Taoism for Jung was that it emphasized working on the microcosm to transform the macrocosm. We must start with small things, ourselves, and work outwards.

> Cultivate Virtue in yourself,
> and Virtue will be real.
> Cultivate it in the family,
> and Virtue will abound.
> Cultivate it in the village,
> and Virtue will grow.
> Cultivate it in the nation,
> and Virtue will be bountiful.
> Cultivate it in the universe,
> and Virtue will be everywhere.[4]

Similar ideas to Taoist philosophy are found in many esoteric Western traditions. The way of the Tao can be symbolized by the tarot card of the Hermit.

> Those that know me are few;
> those that abuse me are many.
> Therefore the Sage wears rough clothing
> and holds the jewel in his heart.[5]

The *Tao* is a oneness which manifests the created universe by dividing into pairs of opposites – *Yin*, the cold, dark feminine, and *Yang*, the warm, light masculine. All creation is manifested by the interplay of Yin and Yang. Phenomena are transitory and constantly changing. All things are ultimately brought into check and balance. When one of the opposites reaches its greatest strength, the other will begin to reassert itself. This potential for change is hinted at by the dark spot within the bright Yang and the light spot within Yin.

> When Yang has reached its greatest strength, the dark power of *Yin* is born within its depths, for night begins at midday when *Yang* breaks up and begins to change into *Yin*.[6]

Yin and Yang

SYNCHRONICITY

In 1920, Jung obtained a copy of the Chinese book of wisdom and divination called the *I Ching* or 'Book of Changes'. The *I Ching* is one of *Five Classics* of Chinese thought and possibly the oldest in the Taoist tradition. Jung's astrological and alchemical researches had convinced him of the reality of the Hermetic maxim: 'As above, so below'. The *I Ching's* divination system reinforced this idea. When consulting the oracle, one must have an attitude of respect.

> *The Changes* is a book,
> from which one may not hold aloof.
> Its Tao is forever changing –
> alteration, movement without rest,
> flowing through the six empty places;
> rising and sinking without fixed law,
> firm and yielding transform each other.
> They cannot be confined with a rule;
> it is only change that is at work here.
>
> First take up the words,
> ponder their meaning,
> then the fixed rules reveal themselves.
> But if you are not the right man,
> the meaning will not manifest itself to you.[7]

The sage performs a divination by throwing yarrow stalks into the air and looking at the pattern made when they fall. Yin and Yang are each represented in the groups of three lines of different pattern, a trigram. Within each trigram, each line may be static or moving. Two trigrams together forms a hexagram. All the possible permutations of the Yin and Yang trigrams with either static or moving lines produce 64 different hexagrams. With each of the 64 hexagrams are interpretations written by the revered sage Confucius and his followers. These elaborate and comment on the text. During a summer break, Jung began experimenting with the *I Ching*. He could not obtain the traditional yarrow stalks, so he cut himself some reeds and sat for hours under a hundred-year-old pear tree practising divination.

Generally, the *I Ching* does not give precise predictions but indicates the possibilities inherent in a situation; but sometimes the answers can be startlingly literal. Jung first tried divination on himself. As he became more proficient, he sometimes did divinations for his patients. One case he recalled where the answer was astonishingly accurate was that of a young man who had been very dominated by his mother. He had met a young woman whom he wanted to marry but was afraid that he might again come too strongly under the influence of a powerful woman. Jung performed the divination and the answer was clear. It was hexagram 44 which is known as *Kou* 'Coming to meet'.

Coming to meet. The maiden is powerful.
One should not marry such a maiden

The hexagram Kou and its interpretation

In the 1920s, Jung gained further knowledge of Chinese tradition when he met the Estonian Count Herman Keyserling (1880–1947). Count Keyserling was an unusual man who began to explore philosophy and metaphysics after almost dying in a duel in 1900. Duelling continued to flourish amongst German-speaking aristocrats long after it had died out elsewhere. Keyserling is known less in the English-speaking world, but he had considerable influence as a guru figure in Central Europe in the period immediately after the First World War. Like Jung, Count Keyserling believed that Western society was in need of spiritual regeneration and he looked to a synthesis of Eastern and Western thought to provide it.

In 1920 Count Keyserling set up a School of Wisdom, at Darmstadt. He brought in lecturers to provide teaching on Eastern traditions. One of the most prominent of these was Richard Wilhelm (1873–1930), a famous German expert on Chinese religion and culture and a former Christian lay missionary in China. Richard Wilhelm had led an adventurous life. During the First World War, he was in charge of the Chinese Red Cross during the Japanese siege of Tsingtao. His relationship with Christianity was ambiguous – he prided himself on never having converted a single Chinese. It seemed rather that the Chinese had, in all but name, converted him. Jung met Richard Wilhelm in 1922 at Darmstadt. Many meetings between the two men followed, during which they spent much time experimenting with the *I Ching* and discussing Chinese spirituality. Richard Wilhelm also lectured to Jung's Zürich Psychological Club. It was Wilhelm's ability to empathize with another culture that enabled him to undertake the difficult task of translating a work of Chinese spirituality into a European language.

Jung's researches into divination systems such as astrology and the *I Ching* were influential in developing one of his most famous ideas – that of *synchronicity*. Another important influence was not Western or Eastern mysticism but something equally mysterious – quantum physics. In 1912, Jung attended a lecture by the physicist and genius Albert Einstein and subsequently met him a few times socially. It was his contact with Einstein that led Jung to make friends with the Nobel prize-winning physicist Wolfgang Pauli, a major contributor to development of quantum physics, and famous for the 'exclusion principle' of electrons in quantum theory. Pauli believed that Jung's idea of synchronicity was heralded in quantum theory, which he believed would lead to a major revision of our idea of linear time. Pauli convinced the equally-famous scientist Werner Heisenberg to take an interest in synchronicity. Heisenberg was interested in a concept so close to aspects of Eastern philosophy. Heisenberg came to believe later that it was the similarity between the principles of quantum physics and ideas in Far Eastern spirituality that enabled Japan to make such great scientific contributions to theoretical physics in the period following the Second World War. The Austrian physicist Dr Fritjof Capra has explored these connections further in his famous book *The Tao of Physics*.[8]

Many years later, when Richard Wilhelm's German translation of the *I Ching* was translated into English, Jung wrote the introduction. In this he challenged the Western idea of cause and effect. Earlier physics developed by Isaac Newton views the world as composed of material entities governed by immutable causal laws. Human action is thought to be explicable in similar terms. Synchronicity proposes a complementary view – that the laws of physics are not absolutes but represent a statistical probability. This is the reality of the *I Ching*. The whole cannot be reduced to parts and everything is interconnected with everything else. To we who live in the post-modernist world, the idea of interconnectedness seems commonplace, but in the West at that period this was way ahead of its time. It is only now that popular understanding is beginning to grasp its full significance.

Jung's meeting with Richard Wilhelm proved to be a major breakthrough in the development not only of his ideas about synchronicity, but of other aspects of his thought. Synchronistic events often occurred in Jung's life. In 1928, he drew a mandala with a golden castle at the centre. For some reason it struck him as looking very Chinese; although there was nothing obviously Chinese about it. Shortly afterwards, Wilhelm sent Jung the manuscript of a thousand-year-old Chinese Taoist alchemical text called *The Secret of the Golden Flower*. The text is concerned with finding the *Chin-jo* or 'golden juice', the elixir of life. In it, Jung found ideas startlingly like those that appeared in his patients' dreams, images and fantasies. Jung believed he now had definite evidence that the human psyche had a common root that transcended differences between cultures. He no longer felt isolated in his quest to understand the human psyche. The Chinese sages had been there before him. *The Secret of the Golden Flower* confirmed for Jung some important ideas. The psyche was real. Consciousness was linked to the body, but it was not totally dependent on it. The exploration, cultivation and development of the psyche was a supremely meaningful vocation for humankind. We must understand ourselves not only in terms of our individual past but in terms of the collective unconscious – inherited patterns of psychological and physical behaviour.

Most of Jung's letters between 1927 and 1930 were to Count Keyserling and Richard Wilhelm. Since his break with Freud, he had felt intellectually isolated. No one since Freud had given him new stimulus or provided keys that would open doors in the mysterious castle of the psyche. In 1930, Richard Wilhelm died. This was a great blow to Jung. Jung considered his meeting with Richard Wilhelm to be one of the most significant events of his life. He believed he had received more from him than from any other man. This may seem strange given the influence Freud had upon Jung, but when he met Richard Wilhelm, Jung felt that his researches into the psyche had reached a dead end. Apart from the surviving works of the Gnostics and alchemists, Jung had found no parallel system for describing the psyche other than his own. Wilhelm provided new inspiration. Jung felt that Wilhelm had died prematurely and that his death had been caused by a psychological conflict between his Western background and religion and his almost complete absorption into the ways of the East.

Jung received a premonition of Wilhelm's death. He was just about to fall asleep, when it seemed that an old Chinese man in a dark blue gown stood at the end of his bed. He bowed as though giving a message and then disappeared.

HINDUISM

Richard Wilhelm's death ended Jung's Chinese explorations for a period. In the 1930s, as he began to approach his sixties, his mind turned to Eastern traditions slightly nearer home – those of India. The main spiritual tradition of India is called by Westerners, Hinduism. Hindus themselves call it *sanatana dharma* or 'eternal law'. It has existed for over five thousand years, a period matched only by the unbroken cultural development of China. Hinduism has a multiplicity of male and female deities. These may be interpreted as real beings or as symbols, according to the worshipper's own experience and understanding. The main sacred texts are the *Upanishads* and the *Vedas*. From the *Vedas* comes the idea that behind the multiplicity of the universe is Unity. This unity is Brahma, the supreme creative force. Brahma is not usually worshipped on an everyday basis. Only one temple exists, in the sacred city of Pushkar in Rajasthan in north-west India. Visitors to Pushkar are welcomed with a sign enjoining them to refrain from the vices of alcohol, meat-eating, hand-holding and photography while in the sacred city. However, Shiva worship, which can involve copious amounts of cannabis, takes place freely. Generally, however, worship in India focuses on deities such as the Great Goddess Mahadevi in her many forms, Kali the Goddess of destruction, and Gods such as Vishnu the creator, Shiva the destroyer, Krishna, a God of divine love with many similarities to the love aspect of Christ, and the luck-bringing elephant-headed Ganesh.

When Jung attended the 1930 gathering of Count Keyserling's School of Wisdom he met a wealthy Dutch woman, Olga Fröbe-Kapteyn. She had been influenced by Anglo-Indian theosophy and was a friend of New Age guru Alice Bailey whose work is continued today through the Lucis Trust. Olga Fröbe-Kapteyn was an interesting woman whose early career was as a circus rider. She impressed Jung as having great intuition and mediumistic abilities. Olga Fröbe-Kapteyn was equally impressed by Jung. She suggested that an annual conference on Jungian studies and related matters should be held on her estate overlooking upper Lake Maggiore near Ascona in Switzerland. The name *Eranos*, a banquet in which participants bring their own contributions, was suggested for the conferences. The format was ambitious – to call together nine or ten of the greatest scholars in the world and to invite people to attend their lectures and discussions. The conferences were exciting gatherings in which Jung was able to present and refine some of his most important ideas. They attracted scholars from such widely-ranging fields as physics, psychology, anthropology, mythology, comparative religion, theology and art history.

The first Eranos conference was on *Yoga and Eastern Meditation*. Yoga is a Hindu practice, the physical side of which consists of assuming certain *asanas* or postures, accompanied by breathing techniques. On a psycho-spiritual level, yoga causes permanent changes of consciousness in its practitioners. In time these may lead to enlightenment and unity with the divine. In the East, yoga is taught by a spiritual guru, but in the West the physical practice is often divorced from the spiritual, and yoga is used as a means of promoting physical health. Jung had practised yoga to calm himself during his *Nekyia* crisis and so was familiar with the physical side of yoga. The Eranos conference aroused his interest in yoga's spirituality. After the first conference, Jung invited Professor Heinrich Zimmer of Heidelberg University to lecture to his Zürich Psychological Club. Heinrich Zimmer was a professor of Sanskrit, the sacred language of Hindu scripture. His lectures showed that there were close parallels between Jung's psychology and Hindu thought. Jung was interested less in Hinduism's religious tradition than in the symbolic processes of change and transformation that the yoga texts described. Yoga seemed to Jung to be expressing the same truths that he had observed in alchemy, whereby the disparate and opposing parts of the psyche were separated out and then reunified.

Jung learned more about yoga, specifically *kundalini* or Tantric yoga, through the work of English writer Arthur Avalon. This was the pen name of Sir John Woodroffe, a colonial magistrate in the British Raj. Sir John's books on kundalini and Tantra became some of the main vehicles through which this tradition became known in the West. *Kundalini* in Sanskrit tradition is the 'serpent power'. Yoga seeks to awaken kundalini and raise it through seven energy centres in the body which are called the *chakras* or wheels. There are seven major chakras which relate to different points on the spine and organs in the body.

In 1932, Jung invited another expert on Hinduism, Professor JW Hauer from Tübingen University, to lecture to the Zürich

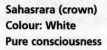

Sahasrara (crown)
Colour: White
Pure consciousness

Ajna (third eye)
Colour: Violet
Pure mind

Visuddi (throat)
Colour: Blue
Element: Ether

Anahata (heart)
Colour: Green
Element: Air

Manipura (solar plexus)
Colour: Yellow
Element: Fire

Svadisthana (sacral)
Colour: Orange
Element: Water

Muladhara (base)
Colour: Red
Element: Earth

Chakra system

PRINCIPLES OF JUNGIAN SPIRITUALITY

Psychological Club on kundalini. The Club members found Professor Hauer's lectures too difficult to understand so Jung followed them up with two lectures of his own. In these he developed his ideas about the links between enlightenment as described in Tantric yoga and his own ideas of individuation.

For Jung, yoga was a means to slacken the grip of the conscious mind on the unconscious. This would allow the individuation process to begin. Jung considered yoga to be an enormous spiritual achievement that represented one of the greatest things the human mind has created. However, despite his respect for Hindu teaching and tradition, Jung had reservations about it. He was no advocate of the 'Go East, young man, and find your guru approach' that became the preoccupation of spiritual seekers in the 1960s and 1970s. Jung was attracted to yoga because it provided a mean of transcending the boundaries of the Ego to attain a higher consciousness in which we are at one with pure cosmic consciousness. However, Jung could not come to terms with the ultimate goal of yoga – the complete absorption of the Ego into *samadhi*. *Samadhi* is a state of consciousness in which all opposites are transcended and union is attained with the divine. For Jung's Western mind, the idea of samadhi seemed a logical impossibility. His intuitive side had never experienced it and his intellect could not understand it. Jung could not conceive of a state in which an individual was at once in union with the cosmos, but at the same time retained a sense of individual identity. It seemed to him that yoga was describing not a state of consciousness, but a state of unconsciousness. If there was no sense of separateness, there could be no 'I' to experience, remember and bring back to consciousness the experience of *samadhi*.

Jung was against an unthinking adoption by Europeans of the more intensive forms of yoga. The aim of intensive yoga practice was to loosen the grip on the unconscious mind. However, the rational Western mind was unprepared for the confrontation with the dark corners of the unconscious that would result. The psyche could be swamped causing delusion and psychosis. He advised Westerners to stick with Western tradition. To those who wanted to use Eastern practices he warned:

> As a rule nothing comes of it except an artificial stultification of our Western intelligence. Of course, if anyone should succeed in giving up Europe from every point of view, and could actually be nothing but a yogi and sit in the lotus position with all the practical and ethical consequences that this entails, evaporating on a gazelle-skin under a dusty banyan tree and ending his days in nameless non-being, then I should have to admit that such a person can understand yoga in the Indian manner.[9]

For Jung the goal of yoga was a kind of 'deep sleep' and an escape from reality. The path to enlightenment lay closer to home. Westerners must find their spirituality through Western traditions. His rejection may have been as much emotional as intellectual. Like many Western spiritual seekers, Jung seems to have harboured a deep romanticism about the East; an East he had never visited. This changed in 1937, when Jung was invited by the British government to India to take part in the twenty-fifth anniversary celebrations of the University of Calcutta. He was to receive honorary doctorates at the universities of Allahbad, Varanasi and Calcutta; three universities that represented Muslim, Hindu and British India. This was an extraordinary achievement for a man who was neither Indian or British and added to the many other honorary doctorates he received in his lifetime from famous universities such as Harvard and Oxford.

Jung decided to take the opportunity of making an extended visit to India and Sri Lanka. He wanted to meet scholars and gurus, to give lectures and to visit some of the famous sacred sites of Hinduism and Buddhism. Despite the slow acclimatization of the voyage from Marseilles in southern France via Suez and Aden to Bombay, it would be fair to say that for Jung India was a culture shock. He did not cope well with the transition from clean, sanitized, orderly Protestant, German-speaking Switzerland to the overwhelming, over-crowded, glorious, disgusting, beautiful and repellent, seething mass of humanity and wandering sacred cows that was India. Jung found many aspects of Indian life irritating and experienced the inevitable disillusionment of the European traveller with over-romantic ideas. Jung was put off by the florid excesses of Hinduism with its glitzy temples and painted deities. Coming from an austere Protestant tradition of white-washed churches, he experienced the same culture shock as does the Protestant on encountering Mediterranean Christianity with its light-up statues of Jesus and simpering lipsticked Madonnas. His impression of India was probably not helped by the fact that he became ill with dysentery and ended up spending ten days in hospital in Calcutta.

There was much in the teaching of Hinduism that Jung could not accept. It seemed to him that Hinduism taught that spiritual progress lay in abandoning the world and turning one's face from reality. He wanted people to engage with the world, not to withdraw from it. He once wrote to an Indian psychiatrist:

> Your standpoint seems to coincide with that of our medieval mystics, who tried to dissolve themselves in God. You all seem to be interested in how to get back to the Self, instead of looking for what the Self wants you to do in the world, where – for the time being at least – we are located, presumably for a certain purpose. The universe does not seem to exist for the sole purpose of man denying or escaping it.[10]

Jung, immersed in his Swiss Protestant Work Ethic, saw the Hindu approach as impractical and possibly anti-social or irresponsible. It seemed to advocate an introversion and self-absorption that were to him both abnormal and narcissistic. He became convinced that there were insurmountable differences between the introversion of the Eastern and the extraversion of the Western psyches. He believed that the West sought to transform the outer world and to make contact with it. The East turned inwards to the world of spirit and the outer world was simply illusion – *Maya*. For Jung, the outer world could not be rejected until we have fulfilled our own personal destiny and done all that we are able to do.

BUDDHISM

Jung found himself much more at home with Buddhism than Hinduism. Buddhism originated in India; although today it is found mainly in South-East Asia, Sri Lanka, Nepal and Tibet. Its founder is the Buddha, a title which means 'the one who knows' or 'the enlightened one'. Buddha was born in the foothills of the Himalayas in northern India about 2,500 years ago. He lived for 80 years. He was born Prince Siddhartha Gautama. It was prophesied at his birth that he would be either a great religious leader or a great king. His father the king preferred the latter. To keep his mind off philosophical matters, the king kept the young prince in a life of luxury; ensuring that he was shielded from the sight of old age and death. One day Prince Siddhartha went out of the palace and met with suffering, illness, misery and death. This radically changed his outlook on life. He wanted to find the answer to life's great questions. At the age of 29, he left his wife and baby son and became a wandering seeker after enlightenment in the Hindu tradition. Buddha spent many years practising extreme ascetic

Hinduism and gained many disciples who hailed him as a guru. However, he later renounced asceticism in favour of the 'Middle Way'. Buddha did not believe in deities, although some forms of Buddhism later incorporated them into their world view.

The aim of Buddhism is not salvation by an external God, but the achievement of an inner state of being – enlightenment. Buddha taught what are known as the Four Noble Truths which are suffering, the origin of suffering – which is craving or desire, the cessation of suffering, and the way to the cessation of suffering. Escaping suffering involves following the Noble Eightfold Path of right understanding, right thought, right speech, right action, right livelihood, right effort, right mindfulness and right concentration. We attach ourselves to the transitory material world which must ultimately fail us. This is overcome by the practice of meditation which teaches us to detach ourselves from the contents of the psyche. Here, Buddhism's goals and methods begin to parallel those of Jungian psychology.

Jung first became interested in Zen Buddhism when writing *Symbols of Transformation* in 1911–12. Zen is the Japanese tradition of Buddhism which was transmitted to Japan by way of China. Zen has had enormous influence on all aspects of Japanese culture from garden design, art, the tea ceremony and calligraphy, to the martial arts. Jung turned to Zen again in the 1930s when he was in his sixties. His friend the Sanskrit professor Heinrich Zimmer showed him DT Suzuki's book *Introduction to Zen Buddhism*. Suzuki trained in Japan, but lived for a long time in the United States and produced a series of books which provided the chief introduction of Zen to the West. Jung was invited to write a foreword to the 1939 edition[11] of the book.

Zen involves long hours of sitting meditation called *Zazen*, in which attaining the correct posture and breathing are a prerequisite. The aim of Zen is *satori* or sudden enlightenment. This is a joyful and ineffable experience of sudden illumination. Like Taoism, Zen does not believe that logical reasoning can show us spiritual truth and many of the exercises of Zen are designed to confound the intellect. Zen teachers give their students as little verbal instruction as possible. Instead, they send them away to meditate upon *koans* which are logical impossibilities. One of the best-known of these is, 'What is the sound of one hand clapping?' *Koans* may take many years to solve. Struggling to find the solution, which is impossible for left brain linear thought, helps the aspirant to deepen concentration and perhaps to attain inner illumination. The student's understanding is examined in formal interviews with the teacher. Wrong answers may result in a loud cry or blow from the teacher. This is not punishment but is designed to startle the aspirant out of his or her mental groove. A proper answer may be a wordless gesture such as the waving of a sleeve or a hand movement. This may not require the teacher's verification because the answer will be so obviously correct.

Satori is considered beyond ordinary comprehension. Here is a satori experience:

> I entered. I lost the boundary of my physical body. I had my skin, of course, but I felt I was standing in the center of the cosmos ... I saw people coming toward me, but all were the same man. All were myself. I had never known this world before. I had believed that I was created, but now I must change my opinion: I was never created; I was the cosmos; no individual ... existed.[12]

Jung saw in Zen many parallels to the psychological insights he had found through his therapeutic work. The aim of Zen is to transform consciousness into a higher state; that of psychotherapy is to reorient the psyche and to seek wholeness. The transformatory stages of Zen enlightenment can be symbolized, like those of western alchemy, in picture form. In Zen, the images form a famous series, the ox-herding pictures, which illustrate the spiritual seeker coming into harmony with his or her true nature. These were drawn by the twelfth-century Chinese sage Kakuan and were a development of earlier Taoist ideas.

Unimpeded

In the late 1930s, Jung became familiar with another form of Buddhism, that of Tibet. In recent years, Tibetan Buddhism has become familiar to us through the Dalai Lama and through news broadcasts, documentaries and contemporary films about the plight of the Tibetan people under Chinese rule. Jung wrote psychological commentaries on two classic Tibetan works, the *Tibetan Book of the Dead* and the *Tibetan Book of the Great Liberation*.[13] *The Tibetan Book of the Dead* or *Bardo Thödul* describes what happens to the soul after death and acts as a handbook on how to deal with what we will meet with there. Similar 'Books of the Dead' are found in other cultures with well-developed ideas about the after-life, such as ancient Egypt. The idea of a book to guide the dead was one that Jung himself had already explored when he wrote his Gnostic-inspired work *Seven Sermons for the Dead* in 1916. For Jung, though, *The Tibetan Book of the Dead* seemed to be describing not an Otherworldly journey, but a journey through the unconscious; in other words the journey of individuation. In his 'Psychological Commentary' on the *Tibetan Book of the Dead*, Jung wrote that he found great inspiration in this Buddhist work and that since its publication it had been his constant companion.[14]

During his time in India, Jung visited the *stupas* of Sanchi, near Bhopal, where Buddha preached his Fire Sermon. The stupas are situated on a rocky hill with views far across the plain. They consist of two great hemispherical bowls in which are tombs for relics. They symbolize the four elements of Earth, Air, Fire and Water and a fifth element of Ether, Akasha or Space which contains the other four and is a precursor for their existence. The main stupa at Sanchi is surrounded by a wall with four elaborate gates at the four quarters or cardinal points. At each quarter there is a statue of the Buddha. The pilgrim enters a gate and then walks deosil or clockwise around the stupa chanting at each of the four Buddhas. Once this circumambulation has been completed, the pilgrim enters a second higher circuit. Jung felt the place to be very powerful. He was moved by the Japanese pilgrims at the site, who came in procession striking small gongs and chanting the Buddhist chant, 'Om man padme hum', 'Hail jewel in the lotus'. The jewel in the lotus was for Jung one of the many powerful images of the Self. Jung found himself gripped by something he could not yet fully understand. He had a sudden insight into the nature of Buddha. He realized that Buddha had grasped the dignity and wonder of human consciousness.

Before he returned to Europe, Jung had another powerful experience in a Buddhist temple, this time in Sri Lanka. This was the final part of his journey in the Indian sub-continent. From the port of Colombo, Jung and his party headed up into the cooler hills of the old royal city of Kandy. Here they visited the Dalada-Maligawa Temple dedicated to a sacred relic, the Holy Tooth of Buddha. Jung witnessed an evening ceremony that began with an hour of drumming performed in an outer hall of the temple, the *manapam*, or Hall of Waiting. Five drummers took up position – one in each corner and one in the centre of the hall in front of a golden statue of the Buddha. Another ceremony followed the drumming in which young men and women poured mounds of jasmine flowers in front of the temple altars while chanting a mantra:

This life is as transitory as the beauty of these flowers;
may my guiding spirit share the merit of this offering with me.[15]

The drumming seemed to speak to Jung, not through the mind but through the belly and solar plexus. It was not prayer to a God or an adoration of a long-dead Buddha but a deep form of meditation that was a healing act and celebration of life itself.

There is much in Buddhism that attracts Western intellectuals such as Jung. Buddhism is a spiritual philosophy that requires no belief in deity. It is an ancient but at the same time modern spirituality that appeals to sceptical Westerners who cannot accept traditional religious beliefs. The Buddhist emphasis is on experience rather than doctrine, dogma and authority. The Buddhist is urged to trust his or her own viewpoint rather than that of religious authorities. Jung saw the Buddhist approach as parallel to his own in its reliance on empirical facts. Buddhism also appealed to Jung's independence. The onus is on us to transform ourselves, rather than relying on the intervention of an external deity. The answer lies within and the 'Buddha-nature' is in everyone. Jung believed that the discourses of Buddha had much to offer Westerners. They showed a means of purifying the psyche and can be a helpful training for those who are unmoved by Christian ritual.

A major difficulty for Jung, however, was Buddhism's attitude to suffering. There are two major traditions within Buddhism, the *Mahayana* or 'greater vehicle or raft' and the *Hinayana* or 'lesser vehicle or raft'. In both traditions the teachings are vehicles which help us on our spiritual journey. Once we have reached our goal, we discard them. The Mahayana tradition includes Tibetan Buddhism and is the most widely practised tradition today. Hinayana exists mainly in Sri Lanka and is closer to original Buddhist thought. The spiritual goal of Hinayana Buddhism is the achievement of *nirvana* – a spiritual state of illumination and bliss that releases us from suffering, death, karma and the necessity of rebirth. Rather than renouncing the world as Hinayana Buddhism does, Mahayana Buddhism teaches that pain and suffering are due to the illusionary nature of our understanding. Mahayana espouses the *Way of the Bodhisattva*. The seeker decides to forgo nirvana in order to assist in the salvation of others. It is easy to see the appeal to the doctor in Jung of the Way of the Bodhisattva. However, the Mahayana Buddhist interpretation of suffering and evil as illusions that could be overcome was a stumbling block for Jung. Working as he did with people who were sick, in distress and often wracked by guilt for past wrong-doings, it was important for him to find a way to help them. Buddhism did offer a way. Buddha holds out hope of complete liberation from suffering by developing our consciousness. Jung saw this as unrealistic. He saw suffering as part of life and unavoidable. The role of both spirituality and psychology was to help the individual deal with it. He wrote in a letter:

> The Oriental wants to get rid of suffering by casting it off. Western man tries to suppress suffering with drugs. But suffering has to be overcome, and the only way to overcome it is to endure it.[16]

Jung began to feel that his destiny lay not in the East, but in the West. Perhaps unconsciously Jung had sensed that he would not be able to relate to India. On the voyage there he spent his time immersed in a seventeenth-century alchemical text rather than guide books of India or reading that would prepare him to discuss Hindu and Buddhist philosophy. Interestingly, he also avoided meeting most advanced Hindu teachers and practitioners. He talked with the spiritual teacher of the Maharajah of Mysore, whose guest he was; but he avoided meeting other gurus. Just as Jung could not accept Freud as his teacher and guru for long, he was too proud and independent to accept spiritual teaching from others. Whether for better or worse, something forced him to forge his own path.

When he came out of hospital in Calcutta, Jung returned to his hotel and had a powerful dream with an important message that led him not to sacred India but to sacred Albion. Jung dreamt that he was with some friends from Zürich on an unknown island which he thought must be off the south coast of England. He was standing outside in the courtyard of a Medieval castle. He knew it to be the Castle of the Grail. Within the castle he could see a tall-columned hall that seemed warm and inviting. Suddenly he and his friends found themselves outside the castle in a treeless rocky landscape. Jung realized that the Grail was not yet in the castle and that something had to be done about it because there was to be a Grail celebration that evening. He and his party tramped northwards to seek for the Grail. Night fell as they reached a stretch of water. Jung realized that the island was almost divided in two by a wide inlet from the sea. There was no bridge or boat. Exhausted by the long journey, one by one his companions fell asleep, until only he was left. There was no other solution: he would have to swim the channel alone to fetch the Grail. At this point he woke up.

Here was a dream full of archetypal imagery and a direct message from the unconscious. Jung still had a great deal to do and his life's work was not yet fulfilled. He must return to Europe. The dream had shown him that 'India was not my task, but only part of the way,'[17] although it was destined to take him nearer his goal. Jung returned to Europe and immersed himself in his studies of alchemy once more. This led to a re-examination of the Christianity of his youth, an exercise that Christians of his time found both inspiring and threatening. Jung's psychological analysis of Christianity was that it was spiritually deficient; and he believed he knew the solution.

NOTES

1   Carl G Jung, *Letters*, Vol 1, G Adler ed, RFC Hull trans, Princeton University Press, 1973, page 113.

2   Quoted in Carl G Jung, *The Collected Works of CG Jung*, Vol 6,

Psychological Types, Routledge & Kegan Paul, London, 2nd ed, 1971, page 214.

3 *Psychological Types*, page 214.

4 Lao Tsu, *Tao Te Ching*, Gia-Fu Feng and Jane English trans, Wildwood House, Aldershot, 1972.

5 *Tao Te Ching*.

6 Carl G Jung, *The Collected Works of CG Jung*, Vol 13, *Alchemical Studies*, Routledge & Kegan Paul, London, 1967 ed, page 13.

7 Richard Wilhelm ed, *I Ching* or *Book of Changes*, Cary F Baynes, trans, Routledge & Kegan Paul, London, 1968 ed, pages 348–9.

8 Fritjof Capra, *The Tao of Physics*, Wildwood House, 1975.

9 Carl G Jung, *The Collected Works of CG Jung*, Vol 11, *Psychology and Religion: West and East*, Routledge & Kegan Paul, London, 2nd ed, 1968, page 568.

10 J Marvin Spiegelman and Arwind U Vasavada, *Hinduism and Jungian Psychology*, Falcon Press, Los Angeles and Phoenix, 1987, page 193.

11 Foreword to DT Suzuki's *Introduction to Zen Buddhism* (1939) in Carl G Jung, *The Collected Works of CG Jung*, Vol 11, *Psychology and Religion: West and East*, Routledge & Kegan Paul, London, 2nd ed, 1968.

12 Huston Smith, *The Religions of Man*, Harper & Row, NY, 1958, page 132.

13 Psychological Commentary on *The Tibetan Book of the Dead* (1935/1953) and Psychological Commentary on *The Tibetan Book of the Great Liberation* (1939/1954), in Carl G Jung, *The Collected Works of CG Jung*, Vol 11, *Psychology and Religion: West and East*, Routledge & Kegan Paul, London, 2nd ed, 1968.

14 Psychology Commentary on *The Tibetan Book of the Dead* (1935/1953), para 833.

15 *Memories, Dreams and Reflections*, page 314.

16 *Letters I*, page 236.

17 *Memories, Dreams and Reflections*, page 304.

THE JUDAEO-CHRISTIAN
TRADITION

He died in 1961 at the age of eighty-five having created not only a psychology but also his own version of the Christian myth.[1]

Jung wrote his first essay on the psychology of religion[2] in his early years as a psychiatrist during his 'Freudian' period. For Freud, God was a projected father image, a 'big daddy' in the sky who acted as our moral conscience. Children's ideas about God were based on their early relationship with their fathers. They incorporated the love for and yet fear of this seemingly all-powerful male figure. Freud's ideas were developed in the nineteenth century when the role of fathers was often seen as that of disciplinarian and discipline meant physical punishment. Children's feelings for their fathers were ambiguous. Another problem was the Oedipus Complex. The male child was a rival with his father for his mother's affections. Jealousy, love and fear combined in a potent brew which was projected onto the spiritual father – the Judaeo-Christian God.

For Jung, this attempt to rationalize the divine simply did not work. Jung had two conflicting tendencies: one intellectual and scientific (his thinking function) and the other an instinctive spiritual side (his intuition). While on an intellectual level Jung could subscribe to Freud's ideas, his own spiritual life told him something different. From early on, the importance of the spiritual realm was evident to him. In his youth, despite his rejection of traditional religion, Jung wrote to a young clergyman that all his thoughts circled around God like planets and were irresistibly attracted to him. For Jung, the divine was the centre of his inner world and he believed he must listen to its promptings. It was wrong to resist this force. His relationship with Christianity, however, was always ambiguous. His own Christian upbringing had failed to provide him with a meaningful relationship with the divine and much of the portrayal of the God of Christianity was distasteful to him.

> Above all, the killing of a human victim to placate the senseless wrath of a God who had created imperfect beings unable to fulfil his expectations poisoned my whole religion.[3]

THE TRINITY

At the heart of most Western Christian traditions is the idea of a tri-partite God. Christianity is a monotheism which worships only one God – but this one God consists of three different, individual and equal persons. These are the Father God, his son Christ or Jesus who is thought to be have been born on Earth by God impregnating a mortal virgin woman, Mary, and a third figure, the Holy Spirit or Holy Ghost, who is often seen as abstract rather than male or female but is called 'he'. Rather confusingly, Christian religious texts describe the Holy Spirit as being the impregnator of Mary;[4] although the Holy Spirit is not 'God the Father'.

When as a teenager Jung was studying to prepare for confirmation, he was looking forward to his father explaining to him the complex idea of the Christian Trinity. For Jung this symbol was a profound paradox. How could three Gods at the same time be one? This fascinated him and seemed to take him to the heart of the Christian mystery. However, when he and his father reached the section on the Trinity in the *catechism*, a book of Christian doctrine, Jung was rebuffed. 'I can't understand this,' his father confessed and moved quickly on. For Jung, this was shattering. It was as though he had been led to the gates of the Sacred Temple and then turned away.

Like all puzzles that we cannot solve, the mystery of the Trinity nagged away at Jung's unconscious, but it was not until he was in his late sixties that he felt ready to begin lecturing and writing about it. In his essay *A Psychological Approach to the Dogma of the Trinity*,[5] Jung suggests that the Trinity is a symbol which represents the three-part process of development and maturation that occurs within each human being – youth, adulthood and old age. This three-part process expresses itself in myths and rituals, especially those of birth, puberty, marriage and death.

For Jung, the Father God is the authoritarian God whose word must be accepted without question. When we worship a Father God, we worship with the unquestioning love and devotion of children. As children, we accept the norms, values, teachings and laws that we are taught by our religious leaders. When our focus turns to God the Son, this is the stage of spiritual adolescence and 'growing up'. We make a conscious effort to separate ourselves from and perhaps even to oppose the *status quo*. Christ, it must be remembered, was a radical revolutionary figure who wanted to overthrow, or at least reform, the religious traditions and institutions of his time. The Holy Spirit represents a new maturity. When we worship the Father, we are in a state of childish dependence. The stage of the Son God is a stage of adamant independence – radical reform conflicts with the older generation and is suppressed and destroyed.

The third stage is a stage of winning through to transform the authoritarianism of the Father God and to recreate ourselves and society. The young revolutionary gains insight and maturity and realizes that there is a deeper wisdom and spiritual authority than that of the material world; one to which we must all submit. In Jung's view, this brings us to a state of self-critical and humble submission to a higher reality. We turn to the divine within, represented by the Holy Spirit in the Christian tradition, and learn to listen to its voice.

Jung's description of the Trinity hints at what became an important theme in his later thought – that of the *Imago Dei*, the God-image, the image of the divine that we carry within us. Jung began to develop a controversial idea that took him away from Christianity and back to one of his earlier interests – Gnosticism.

AN EVOLVING AND IMPERFECT GOD

In 1952 at the age of 70, Jung published an essay *Answer to Job*[6] which was for Christians one of the most controversial of his writings on religion. At first his American publishers considered it so controversial they refused to publish it. The publishers had misread their market. Once released in the States, *Answer to Job* became a best-seller.

Answer to Job is complex and obscure. It consists of a psychological reinterpretation of the story of Job from the Old Testament[7] of the Bible and seeks to explain the existence of cosmic evil. Jung's understanding of evil is one of his departure points from Christianity. For the Christian, God is all good. God is also the source of all things. Logically, he must be the source of all evil too. However, in Christianity this idea is rejected. Jung set out his own interpretation of the source of evil. This is Jung's version of the story.

Out of oneness and eternal perfection, God creates Heaven and Earth, but from the beginning things go wrong. On the Earth is a paradise of animal and plant life, the Garden of Eden, in which live the first human family – first woman, Eve, and first man, Adam. Eve and Adam have been told by God (here the Father God who is sometimes called Jehovah or Yahweh) that they can eat anything in the Garden of Eden except for one thing – the apples of the Tree of Knowledge. Human curiosity being what it is, the apples assume an immediate importance. The serpent, Satan, otherwise known as the Devil, persuades Eve to eat what is known as 'the forbidden fruit'. Eve in turn persuades her husband Adam to eat the apples. The apples give Eve and Adam the quality of the Tree from which they came – knowledge. The knowledge they gain is self-awareness. They emerge out of their unreflecting animal state to become aware of their own individuality; they become truly human. In learning that 'I exist', they gain the joy of consciousness, but also its pains. They become self-conscious. They realize that they are naked and feel embarrassed. This means they must manufacture clothing; already their wants and needs are multiplying into those that will create a consumer society. They also develop the power of ethical choice. They become aware that some actions are good and others bad. They can now choose between good and evil: they can do wrong. Eve and Adam are cast out of the Garden of Eden by the wrathful Father God and must make their own way in the world. The generations pass and humankind becomes corrupt. Eventually the Father God decides to destroy most of his creation except for the righteous. The world is flooded and only one good man, Noah, and his human and animal companions survive. Society is created anew, but still evil multiplies. Wrong-doing is everywhere.

Then Satan tries one of his most presumptuous temptations. He decides to make mischief in the mind of God. Satan implies to God that Job, who is a good man, is only faithful because life has been easy for him. If tested, he will turn against God like everyone else. God falls for the line. He tells Satan he can do what he likes to Job, providing he does not hurt Job himself. Job's possessions, servants and children are systematically destroyed. Job accepts this as the will of God and does not complain. However, when as a final test Job finds that he has been inflicted head to foot with boils, his resolution cracks. Job asks, 'Why?' Eventually God answers, but only to thunder at Job about his own omnipotence: he is all powerful and can do as he pleases. This is a God who cannot be loved, and is undeserving of love. He can only be feared. On the one hand God wants to be loved by humankind; on the other he behaves like a power-drunk tyrant. Jung implies that God becomes aware of the dilemma.

> Could a suspicion have grown in God that man possesses an infinitely small yet more concentrated light than he, Yahweh, possesses?[8]

Jung sees God developing, changing. The different books of the Old Testament were written across a wide span of historical time. In the centuries between the Old Testament book of Job and the later book of Proverbs, Jung sees a new theme emerging; that of balanced Wisdom represented by the female aspect of the divine in Gnostic thought who is known by the Greek name of Sophia. Proverbs is the reputed sayings of King Solomon of Israel who was famed for his wisdom, as well as for his legendary encounter with the Queen of Sheba. At first favoured by the Biblical God, Solomon later came into conflict with him over his worship of the Goddess Astarte, amongst other things. Solomon's sexual activities and his 700 wives and 300 concubines did not go down well either. In Proverbs, Wisdom is hailed as the greatest good.

Happy is the man that findeth Wisdom,
and the man that getteth Understanding.
For the merchandise of it is better than the merchandise of silver,
and the gain thereof than fine gold.
She is more precious than rubies:
and none of the things that thou canst desire are comparable
    unto her.
Length of days is in her right hand;
in her left hand are riches and honour.
Her ways are ways of pleasantness,
and all her paths are peace.
She is a Tree of Life to them that lay hold upon her:
and happy is everyone that retaineth her.[9]

Wisdom, Sophia, compensates for the Father God's tyrannical behaviour by showing the kind and just side of the divine. This signals a change. The Father God wishes to transform himself by becoming human. Mary the mother of Christ is seen as an incarnation of Sophia and is carefully prepared to become the Mother of God. Most people will be familiar with the tragic story of the life of Jesus the Son God and his eventual terrible execution at the hands of Roman soldiers by crucifixion, a form of punishment reserved for those who were not Roman citizens. Just before his death, in torment on the cross, he is described as crying out in despair to his Father in Heaven:

God, My God, why hast thou forsaken me?'[10]

While the Son God is a different person from the Father God, they are also at a deeper level one being. When the Son incarnation experiences this moment of deepest human despair, the Father God at last realizes what he has made Job suffer.

The drama is not yet finished and the fourth and last act has yet to unfold. Jung sees the last act as the terrible upheaval and tumult described in the last book of the New Testament which Protestants call 'Revelations' and which for Catholics is the 'Apocalypse'. These are prophetic writings about the end of the world and are a horrific vision of suffering, divine judgement and wrath. This terrible suffering is unleashed not by Satan but by God. This to Jung was the final outburst of the Shadow, the divine releasing all its pent up anger and frustration with the way creation evolved as the result of human free will. This would result in a destruction much greater than that unleashed by the flood survived by Noah, but the anger would at last be spent. Following waves of destruction, a Sun-woman would appear who would give birth to the Child of Promise once more. A new era would follow in which Sophia, the Divine Feminine or Goddess, would be enthroned with God and a new cycle would emerge. At last masculine destructiveness would be brought into harmony by restoring its balance with the feminine. Some literal interpreters of Christianity and Christian-based cults believe the date of the Apocalypse is around the new millennium, 2,000 CE.

Jung's interpretation of the story of Job could be considered pro-Christian in that Jung sees Christianity as a continuation of the divine revelation which began in the Old Testament. However, Jung's view differs from that of orthodox Christians in that he sees God as a being who is coming to self-knowledge. God himself is going through the individuation process and integrating his own inner feminine and his own Shadow. Jung equates the changing and maturing human idea of God with a changing and maturing God.

NEGATIVITY

One suggestion of Jung's which shocked Christians was that God himself has a Shadow – a negative side. At the human level, Jung's emphasis on the existence of the Shadow and the importance of doing something about it can sit easily with Christianity and other religious traditions which emphasize examination of conscience, acknowledging our own dark impulses, and asking for the help of the divine in transforming them. For Jung the first stage of psychotherapy – acknowledging our own Shadow qualities and deeds – was a spiritual work; for it was only by changing ourselves that the difficult task of changing society for the better could be achieved. Jung often quoted the apocryphal words of Christ:

> Man, if indeed thou knowest what thou doest, thou art blessed: but if thou knowest not, thou art cursed, and a transgressor of the law.[11]

In Jungian psychology and in Christianity, there is a recognition that the Ego cannot succeed without the help of something beyond the Ego. However, whereas a Christian might look to God, Jung taught his patients to look within to the Self, the deeper wise person within us whose viewpoint transcends the short-term demands of the Ego. This deeper and wiser aspect of ourselves has a vision that sees further and more clearly than the everyday personality. Operating from the border land between the conscious and unconscious mind, it has an awareness not only of where we are now and where we have been, but where we are going. The Self is purposeful. It knows where our life's pattern is unfolding and is there to assist us.

On the spiritual quest, it is essential to admit that we cannot achieve everything through the will of the Ego. We must take heed of the wiser person within us who speaks through the voice of intuition and symbol. We must take time for silence, contemplation and stillness. We must look into the night time world of dream by the light of the lantern of wisdom. Hidden within the dream world are symbols and messages that tell us what the Self requires of us. We stop trying to solve all the world's problems ourselves. Perhaps what is more important, we grasp that thinking and reason alone will not help us transform ourselves and others. We need the insights of spiritual wisdom. We must transform the evil and negativity within ourselves, as well as that in the outer world. This is the lesson that has been learned by those, such as Gandhi's followers in the liberation of India and today's environmental protesters, who engage in peaceful protest and passive resistance to evil. We begin to transform ourselves as the first stage of transforming the universe.

CHRIST

For Jung, Christ was an image of what we could become when we became truly ourselves at the end of the journey of individuation.

> He is in us and we in him. His kingdom is the pearl of great price, the treasure buried in the field, the grain of mustard seed which will become a great tree, and the heavenly city. As Christ is in us, so also is his heavenly kingdom. These few, familiar references should be sufficient to make the psychological position of the Christ symbol quite clear. Christ exemplifies the archetype of the Self.[12]

Other images of the Self can to be found amongst the great leaders of other spiritual traditions such as Buddha.

According to Christian Gnostics, Christ was the *Anthropos*, Primal Man, who comes from the perfect oneness of the pleroma with redeeming mystical knowledge. Alchemists paralleled Christ with the Philosopher's Stone, the great treasure created at the end of the alchemical process. Just as God sent his Son to the world as a living sacrifice, so too does the Self send forth the Ego to incarnate itself in the world. In order for the Ego to return to its original state of unity with the Self, the Ego must give up its position as the centre of consciousness. The crucifixion is symbolic of this giving up: it is the sacrifice we must make to achieve our destiny. The implications are that the Ego is not easily unseated from its control over the psyche. It seeks the reunion but at the same time flees from it. In poetry the images of the Ego's dance with the Self are often of hunted and hunter, target and arrow. The way to reunion is hard and painful. It involves dismemberment, pain, darkness and despair. In this, Christian mysticism begins to parallel the shamanic initiations found in tribal cultures.

Jung's journeys outside Europe had brought him into contact with societies which still practised shamanic traditions which had all but disappeared in Europe. Jung saw shamanism as important in two ways. Shamanism was first of all a healing profession. He saw the therapist's role as having many parallels with the shaman. The initiatory process undergone to become a shaman was also relevant to his psychology.

Who and what are shamans? The origin of the word is Siberian. A shaman is a sacred practitioner whose role is to heal the community of its physical and spiritual ills, and to care for the spiritual well-being of his or her people. All illness is thought to be due to spiritual as well as physical causes. It is the shaman's role to provide physical medicine in terms of herbal and other remedies. He or she must also engage in the much more dangerous pursuit of travelling into the Otherworld, the spirit realm, to identify the spirits or malevolent individuals that are causing the illness and to thwart them. Much of traditional European folk witchcraft was shamanic in its origin and has the same Siberian roots as the spiritual traditions of Native American peoples. The shaman's path is hard. Shamans are often seen in traditional cultures as the conscripts of the Gods rather than volunteers. In many cultures shamans are initiated through an Otherworld journey in which they experience dismemberment and their flesh being stripped away until only their skeleton remains. The shamanic initiate survives this psychological, spiritual and physical trauma and emerges with new powers to heal and to divine into the future. Initiation as a shaman can also be seen as coming about through what we in Western society would call a psychiatric illness or trauma. By undergoing the trauma and surviving, the shaman is considered uniquely qualified to help others to do the same.

Jungian psychology teaches that psychological trauma, crisis and illness can be positive and transformatory. For Jung, the shaman's initiatory experiences of sickness, pain, being torn apart and taken to the threshold of death, brought him or her to a new plane of consciousness. The process was akin to that symbolized by the Medieval alchemists – disintegration and dissolution leading to a separating out of the individual parts of the psyche and then reintegration into a new whole. In other words, the process of individuation. Individuation was seen by Jung as originally being the prerogative of shamans and others who were in some way chosen and set apart.[13] Jung commented how in ancient Egypt, it was originally only the Pharaoh, the representative of the God Osiris on Earth, who survived death and was reborn into the Otherworld. Over the millennia, the ancient Egyptians came to believe that all those who performed the correct burial rites could be similarly reborn.

Shamanism was not a rebirth into a land beyond death but a rebirth on the Earthly plane. The shaman's initiation brought transformation and psychological rebirth. The shaman returned with magical powers to heal and transform.

Jung believed we were moving towards a new era in which there would be a permanent healing of the division between Ego and Self. Individuation and psycho-spiritual rebirth would be the goal of all. In the new era, the Holy Spirit, the divine within, would be more important than the Son God. One of Christ's promises to his followers was that when he departed someone else would come to guide humankind. This was the third person of the Trinity, the Holy Spirit. In orthodox Christian teachings, Christ was the only human being in whom the divine was incarnated. In the third stage of spiritual evolution, the Holy Spirit would incarnate himself not just in one human being, but in all people. The divine would be in-dwelling in everyone.

CATHOLICISM

While not himself an orthodox Christian, Jung had great admiration for the ritual and symbols of the Catholic Church. In fact, his fascination with Catholicism led many Catholics to suppose that he had a secret longing to convert. Jung did believe that Catholics were better able to understand his writings on religion than were Protestants. However, he had no desire to embrace the Catholic faith. On 22 September 1944,[14] he wrote to a Catholic correspondent, H Irminger, who believed Jung might become a Catholic if only he understood the doctrines better. Jung commented that alchemists and Hindus also courted him, believing that he was really one of them. In fact, Jung was incapable of following any other path than his own. Later Jung wrote an essay *Why I am not a Catholic*.[15] For Jung, the Catholic Church was a doomed organization:

Every totalitarian claim gradually isolates itself because it excludes so many people as 'defectors, lost, fallen, apostate, heretic,' and so forth. ... I hold all confessionalism to be completely unchristian.[16]

By 'confessionalism', Jung meant sectarianism. Freedom was very important to the anti-authoritarian Jung and a religion of infallible Popes and their doctrines would never be one to which he could submit. This is reflected in a dream he once had. He was led by his father to meet 'the highest presence'. His father knelt and touched his forehead to the floor. Jung imitated him as best he could but:

For some reason I could not bring my forehead quite down to the floor – there was perhaps a millimetre to spare. But at least I had made the gesture with him.[17]

On another occasion he wrote:

I have found that modern man has an ineradicable aversion for traditional opinions and inherited truths.[18]

Despite these reservations, Jung with his background in austere Protestantism was fascinated by, and romantic about, Catholic ritual. The centrepiece of Catholicism is the Mass. This is a symbolic re-enactment of the last meal that Christ held with his disciples before his death. The Mass commemorates this and also the sacrifice that Christ made of giving up his life through crucifixion. By enduring the pains of crucifixion, traditionally Christ is thought to have appeased the angry Father God and thus reconciled him with humankind. In the Mass, an act of spiritual transformation is thought to take place by which the priest changes unleaven bread and wine into the body and blood of Christ. The devout believer communes with Christ by consuming the transformed bread and wine. In this way, there is a mystical participation in the sacrifice that Christ has made to the Father God.

In his essay, *Transformation Symbolism in the Mass*, Jung describes the sequence of events in the Mass – the Preliminaries, Oblation, Consecration, Communion and Conclusion. Jung also examines similar sacrificial rites found in Pagan religions, and in the work of the alchemists, especially the visions of Zosimos, a Pagan Gnostic and alchemist of the third century CE. Jung believed that the human sacrifice in the Christian story is a later development of the myth found in the Near and Middle East of the dying and resurrecting God who is son of the Great Mother Goddess. Often the God is associated with vegetation or crops, and the myth represents the seasonal cycle of birth, growth, maturation, decline, death and rebirth. These myths were described extensively in the work of Sir James Frazer,[19] an early-twentieth-century anthropologist whose ideas were important in the revival of seasonal celebration found in modern Paganism.

Religious rituals such as the Mass could have a very powerful effect on the psyche. They symbolize the death and rebirth of God, as well as enabling the worshippers to commune with the divine by receiving the divine essence within themselves. By identifying with the dying and reborn deity, we are able to experience inner renewal and 'rebirth'. If such rituals are approached with sincerity and insight into their symbolism, we can achieve a true understanding of the nature of the divine and a step forward in the process of individuation.

> The experience of the Mass is therefore a participation in the transcendence of life, which overcomes all bounds of space and time. It is a moment of eternity in time.[20]

In his essay on the Mass, Jung attempts to explain the true nature of sacrifice – a conscious giving up of something with which we identify, without expecting anything in return. Jung sees this as a symbolic expression of the inner sacrifice that it is necessary to undergo on the journey of individuation. We must sacrifice the Ego – the false idea of what we are – in order to realize a new level of consciousness, that of the Self, who and what we truly are. For Jung everything in the macrocosm, the cosmos, is reflected in the microcosm, the human being. The birth of a new consciousness centred in the Self is a form of spiritual rebirth. It was this spiritual rebirth that the Christian mysteries originally attempted to bring about. This was also the aim of the ancient Pagan mystery traditions, as well as that of alchemy.

JUNG AND THE THEOLOGIANS

Jung wished to demonstrate that there was meaning in spiritual symbols which had become meaningless for many in the scientific era. Hence, for Jung, the Catholic Mass was important because it was a collective participatory experience of the individual human struggle to wholeness and the pain involved – rather than because it represented a mystical and magical transformation of wheat into flesh.

Jung's incursions into the spiritual realm resulted in a great deal of criticism from Christian clerics and theologians who thought he was treading on their territory. Of course, Jung was doing exactly that. His rejoinder was that it was necessary. Conventional religion had failed to provide contemporary human beings with the answers they needed to develop a spiritual path.

I would be only too delighted to leave this anything but easy task to the theologian, were it not that it is just from the theologian that many of my patients come … They are seeking firm ground on which to stand. Since no outward support is of any use to them they must finally discover it in themselves – admittedly the most unlikely place from the rational point of view, but an altogether possible one from the point of view of the unconscious.[21]

Orthodox Christians who read Jung's books were often shocked by what they found. For Jung, the only aspect of the divine that he could meaningfully write about was the divine within – the Self. As a psychologist, he could say that people have an innate tendency to experience the divine. What he could not and would not say was that this inner experience meant that the divine existed in the outer world. The fact that many people experienced an inner voice that they thought of as the voice of God, or felt some kind of spiritual presence in their lives, did not mean that the Christian God, or any other God, was an objective reality. In fact, we could go so far as to say that for Jung it really did not matter whether there was an objective God or not. The fact that people had profound psychological and mystical experiences of the divine that could have a huge impact on their lives, usually for the better, meant that these experiences were valid and meaningful.

His refusal to acknowledge that religious traditions represented literal truths brought Jung into conflict with theologians. Some theologians thought they had found in Jung someone who could provide scientific justification for their doctrines and creeds by uncovering in the unconscious and its archetypes striking parallels to Christian teachings on grace, revelation, the God-Image, atonement and redemption. In this they were naive and doomed to disappointment. Jung's psychology was less overtly hostile to Christianity than Freud's, but his aim was to reconstruct Christian doctrine in ways that seemed to him more psychologically balanced. This was anathema for those for whom such doctrines were God-given absolutes. Jung retorted that he was not a theologian or a philosopher but an empirical scientist and a psychologist. The problem was, if Jung was a 'mere scientist' as he claimed, why was he rewriting and attempting to modernize and improve Christian theology?

Jung was highly critical of most theologians; something that probably did not endear him to them. Jung was decried as a modern Gnostic who emphasized 'knowledge' over 'faith'. Jung was indeed opposed to blind faith. Jung thought that the danger of religion was that it would become institutionalized. Spiritual insight was translated into intellectual creeds and dogmas that lost touch with the original spiritual experiences from which they derived. He thought that this had been his father's situation – intellectual belief without experience of the divine. 'With a truly tragic delusion these theologians fail to see that it is not a matter of proving the existence of the light, but of blind people who do not know that their eyes could see,' he wrote. 'It is high time that we realized that it is pointless to praise the light and preach it if nobody can see it. It is much more needful to teach people the art of seeing.'[22]

Jung's ideas could be seen as favourable to religion. He equated psychological maturity with authentic spiritual experience and believed that the spiritual dimension is a real part of the human psyche that we must not ignore. Jung believed that anyone who has a spiritual dimension to his or her life, 'possesses a great treasure'. It is a source of life, meaning, and beauty, that gives a new splendour to the world and to humankind. He argued that, 'if such experience helps to make life healthier, more beautiful, more complete and more satisfactory to yourself and to those you love, you may safely, say: "This was the Grace of God".'[23]

Jung's language here is that of a mystic and, like many mystics, his vision was frowned upon by religious orthodoxy.

Father John P Dourley, a Catholic priest, Zürich-trained Jungian analyst, and Professor of Religion at Carleton University, Ottawa, comments that, 'Jung's mature psychology came to provide humanity at least potentially with one of its more effective protections against monotheistic faith.'[24] Matters of faith that had been seen as beyond human understanding were now understandable; but in symbolic rather than literal terms. For Jung religion was not a set of beliefs, but an attitude to the cosmos which involved:

> ... a careful consideration and observation of certain dynamic factors that are conceived as 'powers', 'spirits', daemons, gods, laws, ideas, ideals, or whatever name man has given to such factors in his world as he has found powerful, dangerous, or helpful enough to be taken into careful consideration, or grand, beautiful, and meaningful enough to be devoutly worshipped and loved.[25]

This idea was seen as startling by theologians; as was his belief that, 'The world of gods and spirits is truly "nothing but" the collective unconscious inside me.'[26] Jung's ideas seemed to undermine the faith of those who believe that the divine has revealed itself in one 'true' religion and that others are false. Jung believed that no one religious tradition could make definite statements about the spiritual realm. To Jung a spiritual outlook is not about subscribing to a particular creed or belonging to a religious organization. In response to a question from the Reverend David Cox, Jung writes:

> I cannot see why one creed should possess the unique and perfect truth. Each creed claims this prerogative, hence the general disagreement! This is not very helpful. Something must be wrong. I think it is the immodesty of the claim to god-almightiness of the believers, which compensates their inner doubt. Instead of basing

themselves upon immediate experience, they believe in words for want of something better.[27]

As he wrote in one of his later works on alchemy, *Mysterium Coniunctionis*:

> Nothing provides a better demonstration of the extreme uncertainty of metaphysical assertions than their diversity.[28]

We have to trust our experience and make our own judgements, assisted by the wisdom of the Self. Jung wants us to be open to the realm of the intuition which is non-rational, mysterious, and takes us beyond the logic of the philosopher and the instruments of the scientist. Jung speaks about the immanent or in-dwelling aspect of the divine rather than about an external omnipotent God such as the God of Job. The immanent divine is the divine of the Christian mystics and the divine of the East and its meditative paths.

Despite his divergence from Christian theologians, Jung was not aiming to destroy the Christian faith but to help Christians find new meaning in it. He did not believe that Christianity was the 'True Faith', any more than he believed that any spiritual belief system provided all life's answers. However, he did consider Christianity, and particularly Catholicism, to be a suitable path for many in the West.

> I am firmly convinced that a vast number of people belong to the fold of the Catholic Church and nowhere else, because they are most suitably housed there.[29]

For Jung, spiritual experience was caused by the activation of the archetypes within the unconscious, rather than through the intervention of transcendental deities. Many orthodox monotheists found this threatening. He was accused of being an atheist like Freud; but more subtle and insidious in his undermining of religion than Freud had ever been. Jung's response was that as a psychologist he could describe only what is within the psyche – not who or what has put it there. This leaves room for people to graft onto Jung's psychology their own religious beliefs – which many have done.

Fundamentalist Christians can find difficulty with Jung's work, but for many Christians he has been a source of inspiration. By demonstrating the role of the unconscious in spiritual experience, Jung showed new meaning in old doctrines. From the 1980s on, there has been a whole spate of work relating to Jung's thoughts on Christianity. Much, but not all, originates in the United States, where people are more ready to embrace insights from psychology than in Europe. Carmelite priest John Welch in his award-winning book *Spiritual Pilgrims*[30] describes the parallels between Jungian thought and Christian mysticism in the work of Saint Teresa of Avila. Religious studies Professor Wayne G Rollins in *Jung and the Bible*[31] has created a glossary of archetypal symbols that appear in the Bible, e.g. numbers, colours, animals, divine names. He describes how Jungian methods of active imagination – imaginary dialogue with the images and individuals who appear in dream and fantasy – can be applied to Biblical texts. Episcopalian ministers Morton Kelsey and John Sanford who are trained in Jungian psychology have encouraged Christians to examine their dreams as important sources of spiritual insight and to see spiritual practice as an inner journey towards wholeness and meaning. Many of the Christian religious orders have incorporated Jungian psychology into their spiritual retreats. The Myers-Briggs Type Indicator, a personality questionnaire based on Jung's personality theory, is widely used in the retreat movement as a means of helping individuals to understand themselves and to explore their Shadows. It has also been used in work with ministers to help them gain insights into their behaviour and how it might differ from that of their congregations. Christian ministers are often intuitive feeling types and may have difficulty in conveying their insights into the right language for other types. His personality theory has also been used to investigate which prayer and meditative approaches might be most appropriate for different personality types.

Christians have not given up on Jung, even if everything he said does not please them. Similarly, Jung never gave up on Christianity. Rather he believed that it needed to evolve into new forms if it was to be meaningful in the modern world. In his later life he began to synthesize his spiritual explorations across the traditions. Let us now turn to his final vision.

NOTES

1 Fordham, Frieda, *An Introduction to Jung's Psychology*, Pelican, 1966 ed, page 145.

2 'The Significance of the Father in the Destiny of the Individual' (1909/1910) in Carl G Jung, *The Collected Works of CG Jung*, Vol 4, *Freud and Psychoanalysis*, Routledge & Kegan Paul, London, 2nd ed, 1967.

3 'Jung and Religious Belief' in *Psychology and Western Religion* from *The Collected Works of CG Jung*, Vols 11 and 18, Bollingen Series XX, Princeton University Press, 1984, RFC Hull trans, para 1642.

4 Matthew I, v 18, from the *Holy Bible*, revised version, British and Foreign Bible Society, London 1938.

5 'A Psychological Approach to the Dogma of the Trinity' (1942/1948) in Carl G Jung, *The Collected Works of CG Jung*, Vol 11, *Psychology and Religion: West and East*, Routledge & Kegan Paul, London, 2nd ed 1968.

6 *Psychology and Religion: West and East*, pages 355–470.

7 The Old Testament is the first part of the Bible which is drawn from the Jewish faith. The second part of the Bible is called the

122   New Testament and was written in the Christian era. This is accepted by Christians but not by Jews.

8 *Psychology and Religion: West and East*, pages 375–6.

9 Proverbs 3, vv 13–18.

10 Matthew 27, v 46.

11 *Psychology and Religion: West and East*, page 459.

12 Carl G Jung, *The Collected Works of CG Jung*, Vol 9, Part 2, *Aion*, Routledge & Kegan Paul, London, 2nd ed, 1968, pages 69–70.

13 *Psychology and Religion: West and East*, page 448.

14 *Letters* I, page 346.

15 'Why I am not a Catholic' in Carl G Jung, *The Collected Works of CG Jung*, Vol 18, *The Symbolic Life: Miscellaneous Writings*, Routledge & Kegan Paul, London, 1976.

16 'Why I am not a Catholic', para 1466.

17 Carl G Jung, *Memories, Dreams and Reflections*, recorded and edited by Aniela Jaffé and trans by R and C Winston, Fontana Paperback, 1995 ed, page 245.

18 'Psychotherapists or the Clergy' para 516 in *Psychology and Western Religion* from *The Collected Works of CG Jung*, Vols 11 and 18, Bollingen Series XX, Princeton University Press, 1984, RFC Hull trans, page 204.

19 Sir James G Frazer, *The Golden Bough: A Study in Magic and Religion*, abridged ed, Macmillan, London, 1957, originally published 1922.

20 *The Collected Works of CG Jung*, Vol 9, Part 1, *Archetypes and the Collective Unconscious*, Routledge & Kegan Paul, London, 2nd ed, 1968, page 118, para 209.

21 'Introduction to the Religious and Psychological Problem of Alchemy' (1944) in Carl G Jung, *The Collected Works of CG Jung*, Vol 12, *Psychology and Alchemy* Routledge & Kegan Paul, London, 2nd ed, 1970, page 28.

22 *Psychology and Alchemy*, page 13.

23 *Psychology and Religion: West and East*, page 105.

24 John P Dourley, 'In the Shadow of the Monotheisms: Jung's conversations with Buber and White' in Joel Ryce-Menuhin, ed, *Jung and the Monotheisms*, Routledge & Kegan Paul, London, 1993, pages 125–6.

25 *Psychology and Religion: West and East*, page 8.

26 *Letters* vol 1, page 195.

27 *Psychology and Western Religion*, page 281.

28 Carl G Jung, *The Collected Works of CG Jung*, Vol 14, *Mysterium Coniunctionis: An Enquiry into the separation and synthesis of psychic opposites in Alchemy*, Routledge & Kegan Paul, London, 2nd ed, 1970, page 548.

29 *Psychology and Western Religion*, page 215.

30 Father John Welch, O Carm, *Spiritual Pilgrims: Carl Jung and Teresa of Avila*, Paulist Press, NY/Ramsey, 1982.

31 Wayne G Rollins, *Jung and the Bible*, John Knox Press, Atlanta, 1983.

THE FINAL VISION

The afternoon of human life must also have a significance of its own and cannot be merely a pitiful appendage to life's morning. ... Whoever carries over into the afternoon the law of the morning – that is, the aims of nature – must pay for so doing with damage to his soul just as surely as a growing youth who tries to salvage his childish egoism must pay for his social failure.[1]

Perhaps one of the saddest aspects of Jung's later life was that he was never able to effect a reconciliation with Sigmund Freud. Both men were too proud and too strong-minded.

Jung's last indirect contacts with Freud were in 1938 and 1939 just before the outbreak of the Second World War. On 12 March 1938, the Nazis annexed Austria into a new country of Greater Germany. Their atrocities against Jewish people began immediately. Freud was still in Vienna. Jung was under no illusions as to what might happen. As a Jew, Freud was in great danger and escape seemed impossible. His daughter Anna discussed whether suicide might be the best option; a course which Jung later advised to Alice L. Crowley if she was transported to Poland. Jung and Dr Franz Riklin, his cousin's husband and former colleague at the Burghölzi Clinic, acted quickly to try and save Freud and help him leave Austria. They raised US$10,000, a considerable sum of money at that time, from their own money and that of other well-wishers. Riklin's son, Franz Riklin Jr, was resourceful, looked German and was unlikely to be suspected of helping Jews. With the cash hidden in a money belt, he travelled quickly to Vienna. Freud was extremely hostile and refused to be helped by those he saw as his 'enemies'. Riklin was sent away. Fortunately, by mid-May Freud was sufficiently alerted to the danger to be persuaded by others such as Princess Marie Bonaparte that he must flee. The Gestapo were reluctant to cause international outrage by sending such a prominent figure as Freud to a concentration camp and in early June he was allowed to leave for London. At the end of July, Jung was in England to chair a conference in Oxford on psychotherapy and to receive the first Oxford honorary doctorate awarded to a psychotherapist. Jung sent a telegram to Freud from Oxford, but Freud's response was cool. He remained bitter towards Jung until the end.

The Second World War broke out in September 1939 and a breach of Switzerland's neutrality by Germany seemed likely. One of the more bizarre incidents of Jung's life is reputed to have occurred early on in the War. In October 1939 he received a telephone call from one of Hitler's doctors in Munich asking if he would go to Berlin to give Adolf Hitler an informal psychiatric examination. Apparently, the doctor and his colleagues were worried about Hitler's sanity. Jung refused. In May 1940, the German advance through France was halted when the French Vichy government signed a peace agreement. In Switzerland, there were fears that the Nazis might now turn their attentions elsewhere and invade Switzerland. The Swiss authorities telephoned Jung and told him and his family to leave Zürich and flee to the mountains. His name was on a Nazi black list. Like Freud, Jung was offered a choice of exile, in this case to the United States, but Jung refused to leave his homeland.

The years of the Second World War were as difficult for Switzerland as the First World War. Jung was 65 in 1940 and too old to be called up; but he worked as a volunteer doctor at an army camp. Jung also found himself on the fringes of espionage. He was introduced to the American spy master and later head of the CIA, Allen Dulles, who became a close friend. Through his contacts with Dulles, Jung had advance knowledge of the unsuccessful July 1944 plot by German officers to blow up Hitler. He was also privy to some of Dulles' more extravagant plans, including one to kidnap the quantum physicist Werner Heisenberg, Jung's erstwhile collaborator on synchronicity. Jung seemed to have a certain appeal for those in espionage circles. After the War, the novelist Ian Fleming, creator of James Bond, became a visitor and was influenced by Jung's ideas on astrology and numerology.

In 1944 Jung had a heart attack followed by various spells of ill health. This ended his travelling days and he spent more time writing at his lakeside tower in Bollingen. The last fifteen years of his life from 70 to 85 constituted one of his most prolific periods. Jung was still looking for a spiritual way forward for the West. I say 'for the West' because Jung was never presumptuous enough to believe that what worked for people brought up in Western culture would work elsewhere. As much of Western civilization was based on Christian thought, Jung believed this could not be ignored if any renewal of Western spirituality was to take place. However, Jung did not believe this was the case for other cultures.

He continued to write on Christianity and alchemy, publishing some major work. Jung believed that alchemy represented a balancing tradition to what he saw as the excessively patriarchal emphasis in Judaism and Christianity. While the Catholics were still hesitant about the role of the Virgin Mary and the Protestants and Jews were totally patriarchal:

> In philosophical alchemy, on the other hand, the feminine principle plays a role equal to that of the masculine.[2]

Perhaps this was one of the reasons why he wrote in 1959, towards the end of his life, that:

> I loved the Gnostics in spite of everything, because they recognized the necessity of some further *raisonnement*, entirely absent in the Christian cosmos.[3]

He also retained a strong interest in Buddhism and before he died was trying to 'get near to the remarkable psychology of the Buddha himself'.[4] Jung was a great dog lover and he felt that Buddhism had a more genuine feeling for animals than did Christianity.[5] This was important to Jung who daily fed the birds in his Bollingen garden and also the garden snake. The birds were so unafraid of him that one day a tit landed on his head and started to make a nest in his copious white hair. In 1956, Jung acknowledged the immense help and stimulation he had received from Buddhist teachings in a statement made with the German novelist Thomas Mann and the doctor-missionary Albert Schweitzer on the publication of the discourses of Buddha.[6] The Chinese invasion of Tibet in 1959 upset him greatly.

Jung found the image of Christ unfulfilling and lacked the religious faith necessary for Christianity in its fullest sense. Christ's unblemished divinity was a problem for Jung who sought a human model, perhaps one to which he could aspire. For Jung, Buddha seemed much more accessible than Christ, because unlike Christ, Buddha was not a God. He was wholly human, with all the vices and virtues that this entails.

128   Jung had explored a huge range of the spiritual alternatives available to him. It is important to emphasize though that he explored these traditions as a researcher rather than as a practitioner. He never became a Buddhist, Hindu, alchemist or shaman. He never formally left the Swiss Reformed Church of his youth, but he was not a Christian in any traditional sense. Where his vision had taken him was through and beyond the traditions and their differences to reclaim what he saw as important for the spiritual life of the coming Age of Aquarius. He researched the past to find answers for the present and future. He saw that future lying in a reworking of the spiritual traditions that we had inherited from the Ages of Aries and Pisces. Aquarius is one of the few zodiac signs symbolized by a human figure – the Water Bearer. It is the sign of humanity and of intellectual challenge. Jung's vision was essentially an Aquarian and humanist one of humanity transformed and the divine made manifest within each one of us. Jung believed that the 'New Age' of Aquarius would be a turning point in the development of consciousness. In 1956, Carl Jung wrote:

> We are living in what the Greeks call the *kairos* – the right moment – for a 'metamorphosis of the gods', of the fundamental principles and symbols.[7]

For Jung, the myths and symbols of the spiritual traditions pointed the way to important psychological and spiritual truths, but now the old symbols were being reborn in new forms to suit different times and cultures.

> The living spirit grows and even outgrows its earlier forms of expression; it freely chooses the men who proclaim it and in whom it lives. This living spirit is eternally renewed and pursues its goal in manifold and inconceivable ways throughout the

history of mankind. Measured against it, the names and forms which men have given it mean very little; they are only the changing leaves and blossoms on the stem of the eternal tree.[8]

Jung was open-minded in his approach and did not make value judgements about which variety of spirituality was best or most true. His study of the myths and sacred literature of many peoples had led him to believe in the universality of human spiritual experience, but also in the variety of its expressions. He believed firmly in the need for renewal of age-old myths. Humankind could no longer believe in the literal interpretation of many of the world's religious traditions, but this did not mean that there were no important messages within them. The psychologist's role he saw as helping people recover their own inner vision. This would be expressed in the spiritual and cultural symbols with which they were familiar.

> Consequently, I do not permit myself the least judgement as to whether and to what extent it has pleased a metaphysical deity to reveal himself to the devout Jew as he was before the Incarnation, to the Church Fathers as the Trinity, to the Protestants as the one and only Saviour without co-redemptrix and to the present Pope as a saviour with co-redemptrix.[9]

Jung was a cultural relativist. He would have been in sympathy with the Hindu scripture of the *Bhagavad Gita* where the God Krishna says:

> By whatever path a man seek me,
> even so do I welcome him,
> for the paths men take from every side are mine.[10]

Nevertheless, while he believed that all paths are valid, he was not an advocate of the New Age 'spiritual supermarket' approach to spirituality. He did not want us to fall victim to a haphazard medley of superficially understood spiritual practices from a diversity of traditions. He believed that spiritual renewal must come from each society's own cultural and indigenous traditions. A renewed spirituality would have to be rooted in our own cultural past; just as Christianity evolved from Judaism, Greek philosophy and the Pagan mystery cults of the Near and Middle East, and Buddhism evolved from Hinduism.

CULMINATION

> This is my daughter for whose sake men say
> that the Queen of the South came out of the east,
> like the rising dawn,
> in order to hear, understand and behold the wisdom of Solomon.
> Power, Honour, Strength, and Dominion are given into her hand;
> she wears the royal crown of seven glittering stars,
> like a bride adorned for her husband,
> and on her robe is written in golden lettering,
> in Greek, Arabic and Latin:
> 'I am the only Daughter of the Wise, utterly unknown to the foolish.'[11]

Jung's final major work was published just before his wife's death in 1955. It was a work of alchemy, *Mysterium Coniunctionis*.[12] He considered that in this late work, published when he was 80, he was able to complete his investigation into the historical foundations of his spiritual psychology. It was the culmination of his spiritual vision. What was that vision?

For Jung the divine could not be a Trinity as in the Christian formulation. It must be represented by the symbol of wholeness, which for him was fourness – a Quaternity not a Trinity.

Western civilization had evolved from polytheism to monotheism to the trinitarianism of Christianity and now must evolve to a new stage. Jung saw square and four-fold images of all kinds as representing two pairs of opposites held in tension. This is a psychological state of consciousness that, rather than denying and collapsing the inner opposites into a false sense of peace and harmony, would maintain and contain them. The opposites that were fundamental for Jung were masculine and feminine, dark and light.

The inclusion of the feminine in our idea of the Divine was very important to Jung. He remained nominally a Protestant, but he believed that Protestantism's neglect of the feminine left it with, 'The odium of being nothing but a man's religion ... Protestantism has obviously not given sufficient attention to the signs of the times which point to the equality of women.'[13]

Catholicism had gone some way to reconciling itself with the feminine. In 1950, Pope Pius XII proclaimed the dogma of the Assumption of the Blessed Virgin Mary into Heaven. This meant that in Catholic teaching, Mary the Mother of Christ was, like Christ, conceived by a miraculous intervention by God and without her parents having sex. While this might seem an odd prerequisite for holiness to a non-Catholic, it must be remembered that the Catholic Church has strong prejudices against sexuality. Mary's 'immaculate conception' meant that whereas all humankind in Christian teaching is born in a state of what is called 'original sin' (i.e. separation from God caused by Eve and Adam eating the apples of the Tree of Knowledge), Mary was not. This does not make her wholly divine but it does put her on the road to divine status; something which is being pursued by a strong movement within the Catholic Church today. Jung greeted the new doctrine as 'the most important religious event since the reformation'.[14]

While Jung believed the Catholic Church had taken a step in the right direction, the Virgin Mary was only part of the vision that Jung had of the Divine Feminine. For him, the feminine must include the physical and while the new Catholic doctrine took Mary's body into the spiritual realm, it was at the price of divorcing her from sexuality.

Christianity's attitude to sexuality and to the realm of nature was a major stumbling block for Jung. Nature and the divine existed in two separate realms, body opposing spirit. Jung advocated a redefinition of the divine as immanent or in-dwelling in creation. This would thus sanctify the body and nature. There would be no conflict between mature loving sexuality and spirituality; something of considerable personal importance to Jung who had married early only to discover that he was not naturally monogamous. For Jung:

Four signifies the feminine, motherly, physical:
three the masculine, fatherly, spiritual.[15]

By turning the Christian Trinity into a new Quaternity, the earthly and physical would be reconciled with the spiritual.

Jung equated the physical and earthly realm with the feminine and the spiritual realm with the masculine. This was a limited view and it has attracted much criticism from feminists. Jung's vision was flawed, but it is important to remember that he was writing over half a century ago. This is a half century that has seen enormous change in our understanding of men and women. It is also important to remember that, although Jung explored many religious traditions, he was brought up in a misogynist denomination of patriarchal Protestant Christianity and was born in nineteenth-century conservative Switzerland, a country which has only in recent years allowed women to vote. Inevitably, this coloured his thinking. Where he was far ahead of his time was in realizing the importance for twentieth- and twenty-first-century spirituality of the Goddess. The revival of Goddess worship and the incorporation of God the Mother into radical Christian thinking have been two of the most important developments in Western spirituality in the past few decades.

Jung wished to see the feminine incorporated into the divine so that we should have both Goddess and God. This was not all. He also wished to incorporate into the divine the idea of the Shadow. Since Mary is conceived free from sin, her absorption into the divine realm means that no sin is absorbed into the Trinity and the problem of the Shadow remains unresolved. As was obvious from Jung's reading of the story of Job, he did not believe that the divine was wholly good. Jung aligns the Trinity to three of the four functions of the personality; the fourth function being the hidden part of ourselves, the Shadow, which is manifest through the process of individuation. For Jung, the divine itself was evolving into greater wisdom and compassion. In part this would be achieved by incorporating the Divine Feminine into the Godhead. It was also necessary for the Godhead to recognize its own negativity. In symbolic language, the dark and light twins would be reunited. Satan would be reconciled with Christ or, to use the mythology of the ancient Egyptian tradition, Set with Osiris.

Jung's inner quest for enlightenment for himself and others took him through the religious traditions of East and West, past and present. He came to believe that for people to grow to psychological maturity they needed not only to work out their emotional complexities but also to encounter something beyond the everyday world – authentic spiritual experience. This does not mean he wanted us all to become monastic mystics. Jung was very much a modern man seeking to find answers as to how we can live in the world today.

For Jung, then, spirituality was all important. How are we to find this? For Jung, psychology and spirituality are not sharply differentiated. They share the same object – the Self – and the same purpose, which is to lead us towards self-fulfilment. He saw the aim of psychotherapy as a healing of divisions within the psyche. This could only come about by what had been seen hitherto as a spiritual exercise, that of turning inward to examine our own motives, desires, drives, hidden ambitions, and all the currents of energy that unconsciously control us and manipulate our lives. Freud's visionary work, which was continued and developed by Jung, was a cleansing of the psyche. The role of psychology was to help us understand ourselves in order to transform our inner nature so that we are better able to function in the world. By helping us to see and feel clearly the reasons for our fears, phobias, behaviours, compulsions and emotions, we can learn to live in a way that is harmonious with ourselves and with those around us. For Jung psychotherapy was spiritual work, and spiritual work required a turning inward to examine the psyche. If we follow our spiritual traditions without turning inward to examine ourselves, we are likely to practise only a hypocritical parody of spirituality.

This leads us to the spiritual traditions. As I have said, Jung made no value judgements between them: except, with his usual tact, to tell their followers that all were flawed. However, he did urge us to turn inward and seek spiritual experience. He provided no prescribed route to this. His map was a psychological one which was designed to help us prepare ourselves to follow a spiritual path. The path must be of our own seeking and choosing. However, we do have a guide – if only we know where to look. Jung believed that the psyche was purposeful; that we have a natural urge to grow to wholeness. Whatever trauma may happen to us, there is something within that remains whole, beautiful and true. This is the divine seed within us which Jung called the Self. The Self is our true guru and inner guide. It is that which in Christianity was called the Holy Guardian Angel. It is the inner voice of wise counsel. Through it speak the Gods.

LAST DAYS

Jung believed that the human life span would not have extended to 70 or 80 years to no purpose. In his fifties, he wrote that what he called the 'afternoon of life' must have a significance of its own and 'cannot be merely a pitiful appendage to life's morning'.[16] The significance of the second half of life was to turn inwards to realize the Self. This would prepare us for the great transition of death.

> Truly the blessèd gods have proclaimed a most beautiful secret:
> death comes not as a curse, but as a blessing to men.[17]

Survival after death was an interest of Jung's from the days of his youthful researches into mediumship. He had no definite evidence about survival, but he thought belief in an afterlife helped us live our earthly existence. It meant that beyond physical life there was a goal towards to which we can strive. To shrink away from death was unhealthy and would rob the second half of life of its purpose.

> When I live in a house which I know will fall about my head within the next two weeks, all my vital functions will be impaired by this thought; but if on the contrary I feel myself to be safe, I can dwell there in a normal and comfortable way. From the standpoint of psychotherapy it would therefore be desirable to think of death as only a transition – one part of a life-process whose extent and duration escape our knowledge.[18]

Jung did not believe in a Christian afterlife. His ideas owed more to Buddhism. He believed in the possibility of our living more than once and that we might inherit *karma*, not so much in the sense of a negative bank balance of past misdeeds, but a psychological and spiritual inheritance of characteristics such as predisposition to disease, traits of character and special gifts. In just the same way as we might inherit physical characteristics, so we might inherit certain psycho-spiritual characteristics.

Jung was uncertain whether he believed in reincarnation in the sense of the continuation of the personality. He often commented that he could well imagine that he had lived in former centuries and had returned to his current life to continue the work he had begun in the past. His strong attraction to England and the English language might have been because he was English in a former life. However, Jung's vision seems closer at times to that of *metempsychosis* or transmigration of souls: our lives are prolonged by passing through a number of different bodily existences, but the personality may not endure. It is as though our life force is undying, but that which we think of as 'I' may not survive. This belief is found in Western tradition. Julius Caesar wrote that the Druids were believers in *metempsychosis* and that the spirit could pass between different species – say from human to tree. Jung had strong bonds with the natural world and seemed able to fuse with the greater creation outside himself. He wrote that at his Tower in Bollingen:

> At times I feel as if I am spread out over the landscape and inside things, and am myself living in every tree, in the splashing of the waves, in the clouds and the animals that come and go, in the procession of the seasons. There is nothing in the Tower that has not grown into its own form over the decades, nothing with which I am not linked. Here everything has its history, and mine;

Here Jung sounds more Taoist, Druid or pantheist than anything else.

As time went on, many people came to see Jung as a guru
figure with answers to all life's questions. In Switzerland, his
opinion was sought by the press, professional bodies and the
authorities on all kinds of subjects including education and,
in 1959, whether women should have the vote. Conservative
Switzerland was only just beginning to bring itself into the
modern world and it was a long time before all parts of
Switzerland enfranchized women. Jung responded robustly
that there was no valid argument for women not having the
vote and voting would certainly not 'masculinize' them, as
some Swiss feared.

Being an opinion-former surrounded by flattering admirers
can be seductive and there is no doubt that at times Jung suc-
cumbed to the temptation to live up to the Persona that others
had created for him; that of the 'Wise Old Man'. However, he
did not want to found 'Jungianism' and he hoped that no one
would become a 'Jungian' because he was not putting forward
a doctrine to believe in, but describing psychological and spiritual facts as he saw them.[20] Maintaining this stance could be
difficult when confronted with those such as Dr Arwind
Vasavada who describes his first visit to Jung after he arrived in
Zürich from India.

I went to his house on the Seestrasse and waited in a room below.
I heard some steps coming down the stairs after some time. The
door of the waiting room opened. I had expected the same person to take me to Jung who brought me into the room; instead I
saw Jung at the door. It was a surprise and a joy to see the guru

in person for whose *Darshana* (visit) I had travelled thousands of
miles, leaving my home and children. I involuntarily fell flat at
his feet.[21]

Tactfully, Jung helped him up.

Were people projecting too much onto Jung? Many people
saw him as what he himself called a 'Mana-personality', a kind
of contemporary Merlin. A leading analyst and friend Frieda
Fordham wrote:

> Late in life visitors, even those with no special interest in his psy-
> chology, were struck by the sense he conveyed of being a truly
> great man.
>
>   He was tall and proportionately broad, tolerably good-looking
> and, as he matured, striking in appearance; many people found
> him very attractive ...[22]

A biographer Victor Broome wrote:

> There were occasions in his eighties when, meeting Carl Gustav
> Jung on a cold winter day, one encountered a tall, slightly bent
> man wrapped in a full-length, fur-lined dressing-gown with a
> dark skull-cap fitting tightly on the white hair, and it was as if the
> timeless figure of his own mythological creation – the Old Wise
> Man – had materialised in the flesh.[23]

There was no doubt that Jung was learned, wise and charismatic. Sensing the power of his thought, many came to him not
with the more practical questions of life, but wanting him to as
it were see behind the veil and pronounce on everything from
the existence of an afterlife to the existence of God. In a con-
versation with the Jesuit priest Raymond Hostie, Jung once
exclaimed in exasperation, 'It is quite clear that God exists, but

why are people always asking me to prove this psychologically?'[24] Jung, like Buddha, believed it was a waste of time to engage in metaphysical speculation about things that were unknowable. He once wrote that, 'Every statement about the transcendental is to be avoided because it is only a laughable presumption on the part of a human mind unconscious of its limitations.'[25]

Towards the end of his life, he was much fêted in his native land of Switzerland and elsewhere. On his eightieth birthday there were gatherings to honour Jung in London, New York, San Francisco and Calcutta, as well as nearer home in Zürich. Forty of his relatives came for a private birthday party and there was also a formal reception. A number of gifts were presented including an original papyrus given by the C G Jung Institute. This is now known as the *Jung Codex* and consists of four Gnostic writings which were part of thirteen volumes discovered at Khenobskion in Upper Egypt. Jung was deeply moved by the gift but felt that it should be placed with the other volumes in the Coptic Museum in Cairo so that it could be generally available for scholarly research. Jung arranged for the *Codex* to be returned to Egypt, a gesture much appreciated by the Egyptian government.

On the whole, Jung found his old age satisfactory but, in spite of being loved and admired by many, there were times when he believed no one understood what he was trying to say and when criticism seemed intolerable. Although his work was appreciated in his lifetime, like many creative thinkers, his ideas were ahead of their time. It was later, in the 1960s and 1970s when the spiritual quest became the preoccupation of many in the West, that his ideas were most understood and appreciated. Jung also suffered the fate of all those who live long, which is to outlive one's closest friends and partner. At times, he was overcome by loneliness; although the famous and friends still beat a path to his door and he received a vast correspondence.

Jung's long-term mistress Toni Wolff died in 1953. The physical relationship had died out and her role as *inspiratrix* was no longer needed, but she continued to be a regular visitor. In November 1955, his wife Emma died of cancer. Her death was peaceful and painless. Jung called the death of this remarkable woman a 'Royal death', but her loss was a terrible blow. They had been married 53 years and Jung had lost the support of one who had been with him from his youth and stuck with him through thick and thin. She was a noble woman greatly loved and her funeral service was packed to overflowing. After the funeral, the Jungian analysts Frieda and Michael Fordham found Jung in his study weeping and saying over and over again:

'She was a queen! She was a queen!'[26]

Following Emma's death, Jung carved a stone for her at his lakeside tower at Bollingen on which was a Chinese symbol meaning:

She was the foundation of my house.

For Toni, he prepared another stone:

She was the fragrance of the house.[27]

Jung died after a brief illness in his home in Küsnacht, Zürich, on 6 June 1961. Not long before his death, he dreamt that the 'other Bollingen' was complete and ready for habitation. His English housekeeper, the intrepid Miss Ruth Bailey who had first met him when she was travelling in Kenya in 1925, commented that in the final two days before his death, Jung seemed to be in some far country where he saw 'wonderful and beautiful things'.[28] It was time to leave the earthly plane. Jung's death was followed by a violent thunder storm during which lightning struck the lake-side poplar tree at Bollingen under which he used to sit. As befits someone who tried, without always succeeding, to shake off the mantle of guru, Jung's last words to his housekeeper were earthy, not spiritual:

'Let's have a really good red wine tonight'.[29]

Jung did not live to take his final sip of wine, but he had lived his life fully as he wished and life's afternoon had been as fruitful as its morning. He wrote in an essay published in 1930/1:

But we must not forget that only a few people are artists in life; that the art of life is the most distinguished and rarest of all the arts. Whoever succeeded in draining the whole cup with grace? So for many people all too much unlived life remains over – sometimes potentialities which they could never have lived with the best of wills; and so they approach the threshold of old age with unsatisfied claims which inevitably turn their glances backward.[30]

Jung was an artist in life and he had drained his cup. Interestingly, his wife's researches before her death were on the significance of the Grail. She too was a seeker and bearer of the cup of the wine of life.

Jung's funeral service was held at Saint Michael's Reformed Church in Küsnacht three days later. There were three main speakers, the first of whom was the Protestant pastor and family friend Werner Meyer. Pastor Meyer made no reference to Christian beliefs about the afterlife, but instead described the afterlife vision of the seventeenth-century qabalist Christian Knorr von Rosenroth. After von Rosenroth's death he was reputed to have appeared to his daughter in a vision, not as she had seen him in life, but as a small boy. Von Rosenroth describes the spiritual journey that has happened to him since his death. In effect, it is this vision that Meyer sees for Jung:

> But now he himself must go through the last great waters, not only as an explorer and discoverer, but also as one who is explored and discovered. May he in crossing the great water cast himself bravely and gladly into the purifying storms of judgment. And if, in the course of this great examination and rectification, one thing or another ... is cut away, because the passing must yield to the permanent and the part to the whole – Nevertheless, this last excursion into unexplored territories will be the most rewarding ...[31]

ACHIEVEMENTS

Jung's life can be seen as the search of a man for the divine. Not finding this in the outer world, Jung finally sought and found it in the inner world. Jung delved into all the major spiritual traditions–Shamanism, Taoism, Hinduism, Buddhism, Classical Paganism, Gnosticism, Judaism, Christianity and Islam, to show us the universality of the human myth of the spiritual quest for unity with the divine. This was to be achieved by an interior journey; a turning inward to encounter the archetypal forces that govern the personality – the Shadow, Anima, Animus and the Self. Jung spoke of a re-centring of the personality in the Self. This involves freeing ourselves from the unconscious control of the Shadow and Anima/us and learning to use all four functions of the personality – thinking, feeling, sensation and intuition – in an appropriate way. To transform ourselves was spiritual work and necessary for the future of humankind. The inner journey of transformation rather than outer riches and achievement is what makes life meaningful; especially in the second half of life. This is not to avoid the duties and responsibilities of the first half of life, which are to use and develop those talents we have been given and to make our contribution to society.

Jung was open to advances in science. In developing his concept of synchronicity, 'meaningful coincidence', he sought the opinion of quantum physicists. He had experienced the paranormal but saw it as natural rather than supernatural. He believed it was the limitations of our scientific knowledge that restricted our understanding of it. While he believed in paranormal occurrences, these represented for him the latent powers of the psyche and may or may not imply the existence of a spiritual realm. His explorations of synchronicity, the patterning of things, made him open to systems of esoteric thought that involved divination.

For Jung, our deities were symbols of the ineffable divine and it was important that our symbols should reflect our human experience. The gods were archetypes and to create a fully meaningful spirituality, all the archetypes of the collective unconscious must be represented. In examining the deity symbolism of the world's religions, he found much Animus but little Anima, much Solar Hero but little Shadow. He emphasized the importance of the feminine. A religion with God but no Goddess was 'nothing but a man's religion'. The divine is a symbol of aspiration, therefore a deity which has not undergone the same processes of evolution that are brought about by individuation and the integration of the Shadow can never be a complete symbol with which humans can identify. The dark brother who represents the forces of nature and the animal world, the Horned God, must be united with his heavenly and non-material Solar twin.

The archetypes of the collective unconscious are found in all spiritual traditions but it is easier for us to relate to the symbols of our own culture. Jung had reservations about whether spiritual traditions could be fully espoused by those outside their cultures. He was opposed to cultural imperialism by the West, whether in the form of imposing our own culture on others, or by plundering the spiritual treasures of others in order to make up the deficiencies of our own culture. He believed the spiritual void of the West had to be filled from within the Western traditions. However, he also believed that beneath the diversity of cultural symbols, the world's spiritual traditions represented a unity. The emotions aroused and spiritual import conveyed by the Mother aspect of the Goddess have the same root, regardless of whether she is Mahadevi of the Hindus, the Virgin Mary of the Catholics, or Isis of the ancient Egyptians.

When Jung wrote about the East in the 1930s, he saw Eastern and Western spirituality as parallel but separate developments, but there are hints in his later thought that he was beginning to intuit that the gap could be bridged. An example of where this has occurred might be the Saccidananda Ashram in the Shantivanam, the Forest of Peace, in the state of Tamil Nadu in India. This was run until his death in 1993 by Benedictine monk Father Bede Griffiths and is now run by Brother Martin. *Saccidananda* is a Sanskrit word meaning 'Being-Consciousness-Bliss' and is used to describe the Brahma. Bede Griffiths' own spiritual Odyssey took him from Protestantism, to Catholicism and then to a spirituality which broke the boundaries of the traditions. At Saccidananda, the community lives a contemplative life in individual thatched huts, meeting three times a day for readings of the sacred texts of East and West. The emphasis is on development of a spiritual consciousness rather than belief in the dogma of a particular tradition. This focus on the transformation of the inner is perhaps one of which Jung would have approved.

Jung was not a perfect man, but he was a man courageous in pursuing his own vision. Early biographers tended to put him on a pedestal and hail him as the saint of our age. Inevitably, reaction set in and later biographers have taken cheap delight in pointing out his many failings. What they have failed to do is what Jung wanted us all to do, that most simple and yet most difficult task, of accepting others and ourselves for what we are. Jung was an inspiring man. We may share only part or none of his vision, but he can give us the courage to find our own. Jung wrote of himself near the end of his life:

> I am satisfied with the course my life has taken ... I am aston-ished, disappointed, pleased with myself. I am distressed, depressed, rapturous. I am all these things at once, and cannot add up the sum ... In spite of all uncertainties, I feel a solidity underlying all existence and a continuity in my mode of being ... Life is – or has – meaning and meaninglessness. I cherish the anxious hope that meaning will preponderate and win the battle.[32]

Let this be his epitaph.

NOTES

1 Carl G Jung, 'The Stages of Life' (1930/3) in *Modern Man in Search of a Soul*, Routledge & Kegan Paul, London, 1973 ed, first pub-lished 1933, page 125–6.

2 Carl G Jung, *Memories, Dreams and Reflections*, recorded and edited by Aniela Jaffé and trans by R and C Winston, Fontana Paper-backs, 1995 ed, first published in English language 1961, page 228.

3 'Jung and Religious Belief' in *Psychology and Western Religion* from *The Collected Works of CG Jung*, Vols 11 and 18, Bollingen Series XX, Princeton University Press, 1984, RFC Hull trans, para 1642, page 281.

4 Carl G Jung, *Letters* Vol II, ed G Adler, Princeton University Press, 1973, page 548.

5 Carl G Jung, *The Collected Works of CG Jung*, Vol 10, *Civilization in Transition*, Routledge & Kegan Paul, London, 2nd ed, 1968, page 22.

6 Carl G Jung, *The Collected Works of CG Jung*, Vol 18, *The Symbolic Life: Miscellaneous Writings*, Routledge & Kegan Paul, London, 1976, paras 1580 and 1577.

7 Carl G Jung, *The Undiscovered Self (Present and Future)* (1957), Princeton University Press, 1990 ed, para 585.

8 *Psychology and Western Religion*, page 215, para 538.

9 'Religion and Psychology: a reply to Martin Buber', in Carl G Jung, *The Collected Works of CG Jung*, Vol 18, *The Symbolic Life: Miscellaneous Writings*, Routledge & Kegan Paul, London, 1976, pages 666–7, para 1507.

10 Quoted in Joseph Campbell, ed, *The Mysteries: Papers from the Eranos Yearbooks*, Bollingen Series XXX, Vol 2, Princeton University Press, 1955 ed, page xvi.

11 *Art. aurif.*, II, page 294f, *Aurora consurgens*, page 53f, quoted in 'Rex and Regina' in CW14 (1955–6) para 542. The Queen of the South in the Queen of Sheba.

12 Carl G Jung, *The Collected Works of CG Jung*, Vol 14, *Mysterium Coniunctionis: An Enquiry into the separation and synthesis of psychic opposites in Alchemy*, Routledge & Kegan Paul, London, 2nd ed, 1970.

13 Carl G Jung, 'Answer to Job' (1952) in Carl G Jung, *The Collected Works of CG Jung*, Vol 11, *Psychology and Religion: West and East*, Routledge & Kegan Paul, London, 2nd ed, 1968, page 465.

14 'Answer to Job', page 464.

15 'Introduction to the Religious and Psychological Problems of Alchemy' (1944) in Carl G Jung, *The Collected Works of CG Jung*, Vol 12, *Psychology and Alchemy*, Routledge & Kegan Paul, London, 2nd ed, 1970, para 31.

16 Carl G Jung, *Modern Man in Search of a Soul*.

17 Epitaph of an initiate of the Eleusinian Mysteries, quoted in Carl G Jung, *The Collected Works of CG Jung*, Vol 9, Part 1, *Archetypes and the Collective Unconscious*, Routledge & Kegan Paul, London, 2nd ed, 1968, page 115.

18 *Modern Man in Search of a Soul*, page 129.

19 *Memories, Dreams and Reflections*, page 252.

20 ED Cohen, *C G Jung and the Scientific Attitude*, Philosophical Library, New York, 1975, page 138.

21 Arwind Vasavada, 'Meeting Jung' in J Marvin Spiegelman and Arwind U Vasavada, *Hinduism and Jungian Psychology*, Falcon Press, Los Angeles and Phoenix, 1987.

22 Frieda Fordham, *An Introduction to Jung's Psychology*, Pelican, 1966 ed, page 144.

23 Vincent Broome, *Jung: Man and Myth*, Granada Publishing, Saint Albans, 1980 ed, first published 1978, page 13.

24 Father Raymond Hostie SJ, *Religion and the Psychology of Jung*, Sheed and Ward, 1957, page 160n.

25 *Letters*, Vol 2, page 116–7.

26 *Jung: Man and Myth*, page 273.

27 Laurens van der Post, *Jung and the Story of our Time*, Penguin Books, London, 1976, page 178.

28 *Jung: Man and Myth*, page 272.

29 *Jung: Man and Myth*, page 273.

30 *Modern Man in Search of a Soul*, page 127.

31 Anne Conrad Lammers, *In God's Shadow: The Collaboration of Victor White and C G Jung*, Paulist Press, NY, 1994, page 240–1.

32 *Memories, Dreams and Reflections*, page 392.

EXPLORING FURTHER

I f you are interested in Jung's work, how might you explore this further? One way is through reading; another is through experiential work, either alone or in groups, that will allow you to use his ideas yourself.

READING

If you would like to read more, you will be spoiled for choice. Every bookstore with a psychology section will have some of Jung's work and books by others about Jung. The problem is not finding something to read, but where to start. I suggest that you first read more about Jung himself, and then read some of his own writings, followed by writings by others on specific topics that interest you.

JUNG'S LIFE

There are many biographies of Jung, which portray him as everything from semi-divine (Laurens van der Post) to closet Nazi New Age conspirator (Richard Noll). The late Laurens van der Post was adviser to Prince Charles and writer of many books including *Merry Christmas Mr Lawrence*, the film of which starred David Bowie. Laurens van der Post revered Jung so greatly that his biography reads more like a hagiography, the life of a saint. Richard Noll's appraisal is coloured by what appears to be a pathological loathing of Jungian analysts. Neither end of the scale is realistic and reveals as much or more about the psychology of the authors as about Carl Jung; although the wilder flights of fancy can provide some amusing reading.

The best starting point is what Jung had to say about himself.

Carl G Jung, *Memories, Dreams and Reflections*, recorded and edited by Aniela Jaffé and translated by R and C Winston, Fontana Paperback, 1995 edition, first English language edition 1961.

Unfortunately, one of the best biographies is out of print, but you may find it through secondhand book stores.

Vincent Broome, *Jung: Man and Myth*, Granada Publishing, St Albans, 1980 edition; first published 1978.

A later work which takes on board much of Broome's detail is:

Frank McLynn, *Carl Gustav Jung*, St Martin's Press, New York, 1996.

Frank McLynn is a professional biographer, hence the excellent detail, but he is not appreciative of spiritual value systems such as Jung's and at times seems determined to interpret Jung's actions in a negative light.

JUNG'S WORK

There are 18 volumes of Jung's Collected Works, which is too daunting for the beginner. Fortunately, there is also a work which Carl Jung himself began just before his death, *Man and His Symbols*. Jung was approached to write the book by BBC journalist John Freeman who later became British High Commissioner to India and then Ambassador to Washington. *Man and His Symbols* became Jung's first book addressed to the general reader. At first Jung dismissed the idea, but he changed his mind after having a dream in which, instead of sitting in his study and talking to doctors and psychiatrists, he was standing in a public place addressing a multitude of ordinary people who were listening to him with rapt attention. *Man and His Symbols* is a beautifully illustrated book which provides a good introduction to Jung's work. There are also many paperback selections of his writings to use as starting points. Some are listed here.

Carl G Jung, *Four Archetypes*, Ark Paperbacks (Routledge), London, Boston, Melbourne and Sydney, 1972.

Carl G Jung and Marie-Louise von Franz eds, *Man and His Symbols*, Aldus, 1964.

Carl G Jung, *Modern Man in Search of a Soul*, Routledge & Kegan Paul, London, 1973 edition. First published 1933.

Carl G Jung, *The Portable Jung*, Joseph Campbell ed, Penguin, NY, 1976 edition.

WOMEN AND MEN

There are many books which use Jung's ideas to explore male and female development. This is a small selection. For men the best book is Joseph Campbell's. Sylvia Perera and Linda Leonard are specialists in women's psychology. Demaris Wehr is Professor of Psychology of Religion at Boston University and writes a thoughtful analysis of Jung's work from the perspective of feminist theory.

Joseph Campbell, ed, *The Mysteries: Papers from the Eranos Yearbooks*, Bollingen Series XXX, Volume 2, Princeton University Press, 1955 edition.

Linda Schierse Leonard, *The Wounded Woman: Healing the Father–Daughter Relationship*, Shambhala, Boston and London, 1985.

Sylvia Brinton Perera, *Descent to the Goddess: A Way of Initiation for Women*, Inner City Books, Toronto, 1981.

Demaris Wehr, *Jung and Feminism: Liberating Archetypes*, Routledge & Kegan Paul, 1988.

JUNG AND THE WESTERN ESOTERIC TRADITION

Nathan Schwartz-Salant's book is a selection of Jung's writings
on alchemy. Jay Ramsay provides a good introduction to the
field. My book *Wicca* examines Pagan witchcraft tradition from
a Jungian perspective. Sallie Nichols' is a delightful book
explaining individuation through the images of the tarot.
Robert Segal of the religious studies department at Lancaster
University examines Jung's approach to Gnosticism.

Vivianne Crowley, *Wicca: The Old Religion in the New Millennium*, Thorsons, London, 1996.

Sallie Nichols, *Jung and the Tarot*, Weiser, York Beach, Maine, 1980.

Jay Ramsay, *Alchemy: The Art of Transformation*, Thorsons, London, 1997.

Nathan Schwartz-Salant, ed, *C G Jung on Alchemy*, Routledge &
Kegan Paul, London, 1995.

Robert A Segal, ed, *The Gnostic Jung*, Princeton University
Press, Princeton, NJ, 1993.

JUNG AND THE EAST

JJ Clarke's book is a selection of Jung's writings on the East. The
other books relate Jung's thought to Eastern traditions. Marvin
Spiegelman, who is a Jungian analyst, has also written on Jung
and Islam, Judaism, Catholicism and Protestantism.

JJ Clarke, ed, *C G Jung on the East*, Routledge, 1995.

JJ Clarke, *Jung and Eastern Thought*, Routledge, 1994.

Harold Coward, *Jung and Eastern Thought*, SUNY, Albany, NY,
1985.

J Marvin Spiegelman and M Miyuki, *Buddhism and Jungian Psychology*, Falcon Press, Los Angeles and Phoenix, 1985.

J Marvin Spiegelman, and Arwind U Vasavada, *Hinduism and Jungian Psychology*, Falcon Press, Los Angeles and Phoenix, 1987.

JUNG AND CHRISTIANITY

Catholics, High Anglicans and Episcopalians are more familiar with a symbolic approach to Christianity and have been more ready than other traditions to embrace Jung's work. Father Christopher Bryant was an Anglican monk, Wallace Clift is an Episcopalian Minister based in Denver, and Father John Welch is a Carmelite.

Christopher Bryant, *Jung and the Christian Way*, Darton, Longman and Todd, London, 1983.

Wallace B Clift, *Jung and Christianity: The Challenge of Reconciliation*, Crossroad, New York, 1982.

John Welch, O Carm, *Spiritual Pilgrims: Carl Jung and Teresa of Avila*, Paulist Press, NY/Ramsey, 1982.

BEYOND READING

To begin to explore the unconscious using Jung's methods, the best starting point is to attend some lectures, workshops or other events where you can hear Jung's ideas discussed and do some preliminary experiential work. Another option is to undertake full Jungian therapy with an analyst trained by an approved body. This is time consuming and expensive and should not be undertaken lightly. Usually analysis takes place a number of times a week and goes on for a few years. However, for those unable to afford the full fees, some institutes are able to offer reduced fee places with analysts in training.

Workshops on themes related to Jung's work take place in all major cities. You will be able to find local events listed in New Age magazines. Bookstores with large psychology and New Age sections will probably carry leaflets advertising events and/or magazines with advertisements and events listings. Many workshops will use particular creative approaches to explore Jung's work; for instance, art, dream analysis, creative writing, poetry, story-telling and astrology. The Christian retreat movement runs many workshops on Jungian-related themes. Information can be found in many Christian book stores and Catholic religious artefact shops.

Institutes and organizations dedicated to teaching and developing Jung's work exist throughout the world. Here I can only list a small selection of them. As well as providing referral services for those seeking Jungian analysis, many have programmes of lectures and workshops that are open to the public and publish books and journals on Jung's work. If there is no listing for your area, contact one of the institutes in your country to find out if there is a centre near you. If there is no listing for your country, then write to the CG Jung Institute, Zürich, which has addresses of institutes around the world. Alternatively, if you have access to the Internet, you can use the web sites listed below as a starting point.

EUROPE

Aradia Trust runs Vivianne and Chris Crowley's workshops on *Psychology of the Sacred* and on personality type. *Psychology of the Sacred* is a workshop series exploring spiritual psychology and personal development using Jung's ideas as explained in this book and related work. The workshops can provide a qualifying stage for counselling training offered by the Centre for Transpersonal Psychology. The Personality Type workshops are day workshops using the Myers-Briggs Type Indicator (MBTI)®[1]

which reveal your personality type according to Jung's theories and provide insights on how this relates to relationships, vocational choice and spiritual development. One-to-one sessions on the MBTI for career counselling or personal development are available in London. Address: BM DEOSIL, London WC1N 3XX, England. EMail: BMDEOSIL@aol.com

Association of Jungian Analysts, 7 Eton Avenue, London NW3 3EL. Telephone 0171 794 8711.

Belgian School for Jungian Psychoanalysis, 108 rue du Tabellion, B-1050 Brussels, Belgium. Telephone (02) 479 7849 and (02) 534 7007.

British Association of Psychotherapists (Jungian section), 37 Mapesbury Road, London NW2 4HJ, England. Telephone 0181 452 9823.

C.G. Jung Insitut Berlin e.V., Lietzenburgerstrasse 54, D-10719 Berlin-Charlottenburg, Germany. Telephone (030) 886 0792. Fax (030) 886 0773.

C.G. Jung Insitut München e.V., Partenkirchenstrasse 7, 81377 München, Germany. Telephone (089) 714 9854.

C.G. Jung Insitut Stuttgart e.V., Alexanderstrasse 92, 70182 Stuttgart, Germany.

C.G. Jung Institute Zürich, Hornweg 28, CH-8700 Küsnacht, Switzerland. Telephone 01 910 5323, Fax 01 910 5451. This is the original Jungian training institute.

C.G. Jung-Gesellschaft Köln e.V., Kartäuserwall 24b, 50678 Köln, Germany. Telephone/fax 0221 310 1438. EMail: weyer-strass@servicehouse.de.

Centre for Transpersonal Psychology, 7–11 Kensington High Street, London W8 5NP, England. Telephone (0171) 937 9190. This centre was founded by Barbara Somers and the late Ian Gordon-Brown. Workshops and counselling training in the UK and Ireland.

Fachrichtung Analytische Psychologie am Psychoanalytischen Institut Bremen e.V., Am Dobben 21, 28203 Bremen, Germany. Telephone (0421) 32 47 29.

Guild of Pastoral Psychology, PO Box 1107, London W3 6ZP. Telephone (0181) 993 8366. This is not a training institute but a forum for those interested in Jungian psychology and religion and has lectures, seminars and conferences.

Instituto di Milano, Via XX Settembre 11, 20123 Milano, Italy. Telephone (02) 481 5937.

Instituto di Roma, Via Pisanelli 1, 00100 Roma, Italy. Telephone/fax (06) 321 6303.

National Retreat Association, The Central Hall, 256 Bermondsey Street, London SE1 3UJ. Telephone (0171) 357 7736. Publishes *Retreats* magazine (formerly *The Vision*) which lists Christian organizations providing Jungian workshops. *Retreats* can be found in religious bookstores.

Scientific and Medical Network is not a Jungian organization but may be of interest to scientists with Jungian interests. It is an international grouping of scientists, academics, engineers, therapists and medical practitioners who are working to bridge the gap between science and mysticism. It runs interesting conferences and events. Gibliston Mill, Colinsburgh, Leven, Fife, Scotland, KY9 1JS, UK. EMail: SciMedNetwork@compuserve.com

Sociedad Español de Psicologia Analitica, Dr Pere Segura i Ferrer, C/Industria 241, Esq. ent.-3, E-08026 Barcelona, Spain. Telephone (93) 456 0103. Fax (93) 455 8094.

Société Belge de Psychologie Analytique, Av. Dr Castel 12/8, 1200 Bruxelles, Belgium. Telephone (02) 771 7911.

Société Française de Psychologie Analytique, 6 rue Rampon, 75011 Paris, France. Telephone (43) 57 18 26. Fax (43) 57 20 50.

Transpersonal Psychology Study Centre, Bridge House, Culmstock, Cullompton, Devon, England. Telephone (01884)

840515. Founded by Reynold and Joan Swallow, the centre offers workshops and counselling training.

NORTH AND SOUTH AMERICA

Associaco Junguiana do Brasil (AJB), Rua Filadelfo de Azevedo 498, Sao Paulo, SP, Brazil. Telephone 04508 010.

C.G. Jung Foundation, 223 St Clair Avenue West, Toronto, ON M4V 1R3, Canada. Telephone 416 961 9767.

C.G. Jung Foundation, 28 East 39th Street, New York, New York 10016, USA. Telephone (212) 697 6430.

C.G. Jung Institute of Chicago, 1567 Maple Avenue, Evanston, Illinois 60201, USA. Telephone (708) 475 4848. Fax (708) 475 4970.

C.G. Jung Institute of Los Angeles, 10349 West Pico Blvd, Los Angeles, California 90064, USA. Telephone (310) 556 1193. Fax (310) 556 2290.

C.G. Jung Institute of San Francisco, 2040 Gough St, San Francisco, California 94109, USA. Telephone (415) 771 8055. Fax (415) 771 8926.

Endereço do Instituto Junguiano do Rio de Janeiro, Rua Sorocaba, 747/sala 201, 22271-110-Rio de Janeiro, RJ, Brazil. Telephone (021) 527 0932.

Istituto Rio de Janeiro, Rua Almirante Pereira Guimaraes 72, CJ504/505, CEP 22440 Rio de Janeiro, Brazil. Telephone 239 2246.

Jungian Analysts – North Pacific, 2010 Waverley Place North No. 1, Seattle, Washington 98109, USA.

New England Society of Jungian Analysts, 283 Commonwealth Avenue, Boston, Massachusetts 02115, USA. Telephone (617) 267 5984.

Philadelphia Association of Jungian Analysts, 119 Coulter Avenue, Ardmore, Pennsylvania 19003-2427, USA.

Australian and New Zealand Society of Jungian Analysts (ANZS-JA), 8 Mueller St, PO Box 9201, Alice Springs, NT 0871, Australia. Telephone 61 89 517 580. Fax 61 89 517 585. EMail: adekon@tpgi.com.au

South Africa Association of Jungian Analysts, 4 Linray Road, Rosebank, 7700 Cape Town, South Africa. Telephone (021) 685 7871. EMail: saaja@gem.co.za

WEB SITES

There is a vast amount of information about Carl Jung, his works, and Jungian organizations on the Worldwide Web. The addresses below are good starting points. They all have links to other sites. You could also do a search on 'Carl Jung'.

English language:
http://www.cgjung.com/cgjung/linkx.html and
http://www.cgjung.com/institutx.html

German language:
http://www.access.ch/psychonline

NOTE

1 The Myers-Briggs Type Indicator is a registered trademark of Consulting Psychologists Press.